ACCOUNTS IN 1 DAY

Moses Carson B. FCCA, DBA, BA/EDUC

Academy of Practical Accounts LTD, UK

© Copy right

All rights reserved. No part of this publication may be reproduced, stored in a retrieval system, or transmitted in any form, or by any means, electronic, mechanical, photocopying, recording, or otherwise without the written permission of the copyright owner.

FIRST EDITION   JANUARY 2018
SECOND EDITION   FEBRUARY 2018
THIRD EDITION   MARCH 2018

I0481483

Other Books in the Series;

- General Knowledge Bookkeeping & Accounts
- Practical Bookkeeping Theory
- The Practical Accounting Process
- Excel Bookkeeping & Accounting
- Practical & Computerised Accounts Training

Scan the Free Practice App: ➡

FREE SUPPORT via Whatsapp- 0044 7415 618 342

Acknowledgment

Mr Fomba Bernard, HIMS President, Buea, Cameroon
Mr Ntam James, Director, School of Expert Capacity Building, HIMS, Buea, Cameroon

CONTENTS

Chapter 1. **INTRODUCTION**

Objectives To Achieve

A. Recording From Documents
1) Money Capital
2) Adding Stock Items
3) Stock Purchases
4) Stock Sales
5) Point of Sale
6) Cash Deposit
7) Loan Borrowed & Interest
8) Personal Cash Taken
9) Rent Paid
10) Cash Withdraw
11) Fixed Asset
12) Tax Paid

B. Presenting Reports
1) The Ledger - AGL
2) Trial Balance -
3) Stock Information
4) Stock Movement
5) Annual Stock Sales & Profit
6) Stock Taking List
7) Cash Register
8) Notes to Financial Statements
9) Profit and Loss Account
10) Balance Sheet
11) Tax Report
12) Owner's Income Calculation

Who is it For?
1. Trainee Accountants
2. Trainee Bookkeepers
3. Business Owners (DIY)
4. Management (General Understanding)

General Overview
In simple terms, **Bookkeeping is the recording of what a business receives and pays.** Improve this by saying "it's the recording of what a business receives and pays out in money terms, onto accounts and summarising into a Trial Balance. **An account** is a report about a particular business item like Cash, where we record the money value of what was Received and Paid out. **Each business** item has its own report or Account. As we record the **Values,** we also record the Date, a brief explanation or Narration, and the document number. For Tax purposes, what is recorded should be copied from a physical **document**, which is filed and stored to support what is recorded.

Whether Received or Paid Out, each value is recorded on 2 accounts, once on the account which received value (the **account To**), and once on the account which gave value, (the **account From**). So for every recording there **must be** an account which Gives Value, (the **Giver** or **account From**), and an account which receives Value (the **account To**).

As we record value or **money received** on the Cash account, we must make a corresponding record on the Sales account which **gave away the value**. As we record on the Rent Expense account which **receives Value**, we must make a corresponding record on the Cash account which paid **(gave away).** If any value is Not recorded twice then there is an error which is exposed by a difference on the Trial Balance.

However, with this software we select **both** the Receiving (**To**) and Giving (**From**) accounts on the recording form at the same time. And since the software automates the second figure, we don't expect a difference or Trial Balance error.

So **Bookkeeping** involves the **copying** of information from Documents, recording onto Accounts (in the Ledger), and summarising into a Trial Balance.   **A ledger** is the book or collection where we find all the Accounts.

The **Accounting** process prepares **Accounts**, by copying figures from the Trial Balance, to generate the Notes to Financial Statements, and presenting the summarized Profit and Loss Account, and Balance Sheet, as illustrated below. The Profit and Loss account displays the difference between Incomes and Expenses, as **a Profit or a Loss**.

For countries where a **Tax Report or Return** is required from every business, the figures come from the Profit and Loss Account, and Balance Sheet.

Below is an illustration of the Accounting process from documents upto a **Tax Report;**

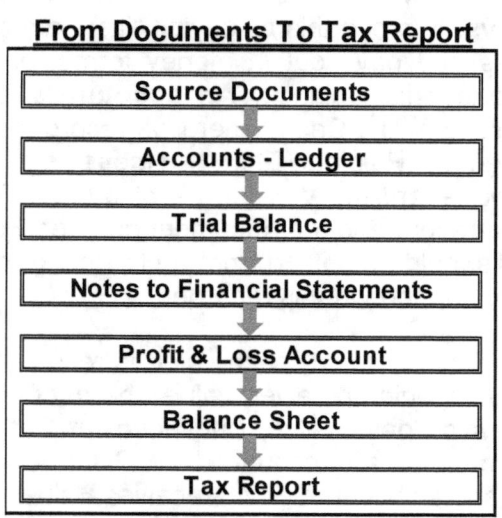

From Documents To Tax Report

| Source Documents |
| Accounts - Ledger |
| Trial Balance |
| Notes to Financial Statements |
| Profit & Loss Account |
| Balance Sheet |
| Tax Report |

Learning Accounts in 1 Day is possible since over 90% of the process is **automated**. This format takes the **shortest period to learn** and **implement**. All you need is an **Android Phone or Tablet**, and will soon be updated on IPhone and IPads. However, you should already be conversant with basics on your Mobile Device, otherwise it takes longer.

The Free App for this approach is: **Free Accounts Module 1**, on Google Play or the Play Store. For those who don't wish to engage in the time consuming exercise of analysing Expenses and Incomes, this is the format to follow.

What is explained in this module is the recording and reporting format for **individual businesses Not Registered for Vat in UK**, and is acceptable elsewhere. In countries where small businesses don't prepare Accounting Records, this simplified format should be preferred and encouraged by authorities, as opposed to nothing. It provides **standard reporting with minimal effort**, which can be **customised** and **localised** further.

All Purchases including Assets are recorded as Expenses to a Single account "**25 All Expenses**". All Income is recorded to a single account "**5 All Income**". This is sufficient for the **3 Line Profit and Loss account** required for reporting to the **Revenue Authority** using the Short Tax Return. A summary **Balance Sheet** is automated, together with **Tax** and **Income** for the business owner. All this is presented on a single report, the "**Dashboard - Overview**".
This training involves the recording of 11 commonly known types of documents and transactions. They are; **Income, Expenses, Capital, Bank Deposit and Withdraw, Loan and Interest, Rent, Personal Cash, Tablet Computer, and Tax Paid.** Since they are known, no time is consumed understanding what they are.

The recording forms to use are prescribed. Some forms are specialised and open with **both required accounts pre-selected**. Some forms open with **only 1 required account pre-selected**. It's only the 2F Multi Use form that requires selecting the 2 accounts.

The Date for most documents is **set once**. All forms open with an **editable document number** and **Narration** (except 2F). All the **Posting** to the Ledger, **Balancing**, and **Reports preparation** are **automated**.
Please Note, although recording is done using a Small Mobile Device, the reports printed are **A4 or customized to A5 and other sizes**. The printing can be done as an ordinary **PDF** via a **PC**, onto an **ordinary Printer**, or straight to a **wireless Printer**.

At this training level we don't look at any of the **23 Period Reports** prepared by the software. We look at the **Annual General Ledger and C1 Final Trial Balance**. Out of **13 Stock Reports** we look at the **ST1** Stock Information, **ST5** Stock Movement, **ST11** Annual Sales and Profit, plus **ST13** Stock Taking List. **Out of 80 Annual Reports**, only the **C1** Final Trial Balance, **B4** Notes to Financial Statements, **B1** Profit and Loss account, **B2** Balance Sheet, and **A1** Short Tax Return are looked at. Plus the **Dashboard**.

No definitions or terminologies to master, just a quick App overview and start recording documents. Open customized forms that come with a date, brief explanation, and 50% of the required accounts. Type the amount, Save, and Display or Print Reports. This can be done for 11 types of documents and transactions within a Day.

The initial objective is learning to record, the understanding of the process can be gradual. This simplified presentation of Accounts encourages Small Business Owners do it themselves (**DIY**).

Assumptions Followed
This format is for a Personal business Not Registered for Vat
All Incomes go to account 5, and all Expenses to account 25
Computers, Other Equipment, and Vehicles used for only 2 years (But Not Cars) are recorded as Expenses
It's all Cash transactions without Credit.
It's on a Receipts basis without Year End Adjustments
All documents are stored on single file.

Document Numbering and Filing
In the simplest filing for a small business, we can have a **single file** for both Income and Expenses. However, the appropriate single file should be a **Box or Spring File** where it's easy to insert documents in the separated sections. Following regular filing, the one at the bottom is among the oldest, while the most recent is at the Top of the pile.

Documents are differentiated using **numbers**. The bottom most document is numbered **1**, and we progress upwards. A distinct colour Pen like **Red** should be used for easier identification. In terms of transaction support explained in Chapter 15, tracing a document on the File is easier.

Software Features and Benefits
The software used on this training format has the following;
An **Offline** App for Mobiles and Tablets
Data is **stored on device**, requires brief Internet for Authentication
Free Support by WhatsApp and Lite Facebook Messenger
Has a **Point of Sale**, Cash Register, **Stocktaking** & Management
Specialised Forms for Quick Recording in Seconds
Prints Receipts, Invoices & Reports
Document numbers automated
Wage Computations Customized and **Pay Slips** Printed
Guides in the "i", on all Recording Forms and Reports
Backup and Restore on another Device
Compare Monthly, Quarterly & Annual Results
Tasks Checklist Integrated
Calculates Weekly, Monthly & Annual **Income**
23 Period Reports, **13** Stock Reports, and **80** Year End Reports
For **unlimited** number of businesses

Other Apps
Although this learning can be accomplished using the **Free App**, the paid
Equivalent is "**Small Business Accounts Suite**", which is used for both
M1 and M2. We also have **Sole Trader Accounts** that is used for **M3,
and M4**. The **differences** with Small Business Accounts are; Vat options,
more customized forms for a variety of documents and transactions
including **Tax Adjustments**, and **a longer Year End Reports Checklist**.

We also have the **Limited Company Accounts App**, used for **modules
5 and 6**. The major differences are; it has **more Accounts** in the General
Ledger, **differentiated Financial Statements**, with a **longer Year End
Reports Checklist.**

Flexpansion Keyboard
Most Android phones have the Android Keyboard pre-installed and works
fine. However, we have found the Flexpansion Keyboard to be more
efficient. Apart from word prediction, it has **4 arrows** that move 1 step
Up, Down, Left & Right**, which eases navigation when editing figures
and text**. It also provides **direct access to numbers** when in the
alphabet option. Their **Free option** serves quite well. Therefore, we
recommend that you install Flexpansion.

Further Training
Although the 11 types of Documents, Transactions, and the few Reports
covered may suffice for a small business owner, it's just a Practical
introduction for an aspiring Bookkeeper or Accountant. For the one

learning to keep their own records, they should at least cover upto **Module 2.** Which covers more types of documents, transactions, analyses Incomes and Expenses, Opening Balances, Previous Year Comparison balances, looks at more Reports, plus **extra practice**. Some **minimal experience** is built, although we continue to provide support.

Below is an illustration of the 6 modules for those aspiring to become an Accounting Technician;

PRACTICAL ACCOUNTS TECHNICIAN
The 6 Modules

1. Accounts in 1 Day : 3 - 6 Hrs	4. Sole Trader Accounting - 50 Hrs - Exam
2. Small Business Accounts: 10 - 15 Hrs Exam	5. Limited Company Bookkeeping-30 Hrs-Exam
3. Sole Trader Bookkeeping - 50 Hrs - Exam	6. Limited Company Accounting - 30 Hrs- Exam

M3 looks at a **Vat registered Sole Trader**, while M4 looks at **Comprehensive Year End Reporting** with about 80 reports. M5 and M6 look at **Limited Company Bookkeeping and Accounting.**

Please Note, this Guide is based on the updated features on the Paid Version. You may find minor differences with the FREE version, but the functionality and reporting don't differ.

Support
In case of any questions please contact us via **WhatsApp** +44 7415 618 342 or **Lite Facebook Messenger, & Facebook** Alternative contacts are; admin@practicalaccounts.com, and mosesbak@yahoo.co.uk

Chapter 2. <u>BRIEF APP OVERVIEW</u>

2.1   Installation

How an App is installed is commonly known. However, the procedure on Android devices is straightforward. Find the App **"Play Store"** on your device. With an Internet connection, Tap to open, type the App Name in the Top search box, "**Free Accounts Module 1**". It may be displayed instantly or scroll down to find it. Tap the **install** button since it's **Free**. Then register and log in with a brief Internet connection. Then start with the overview. The procedure for IOS will be added after updating the App on ITunes.

Next is a brief introductory look at some software modules hosting buttons that lead to those facilities covered in this Accounts in a Day Module. We only look at the bare minimum.

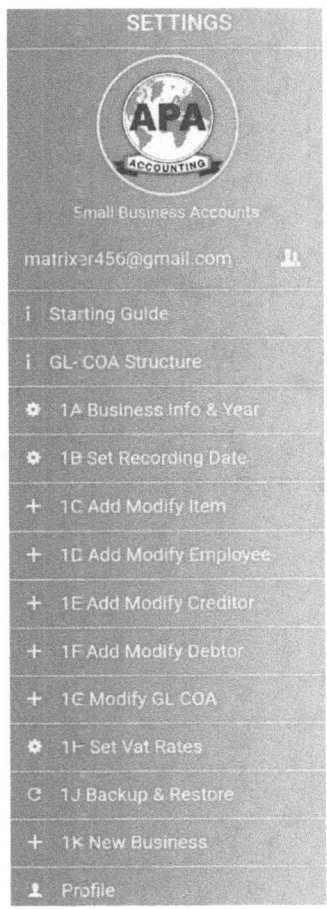

2.2   Settings Menu

This is module 1 which is also the **Side Menu**. It mainly hosts the settings features plus a few others. This is accessed by tapping the 3 white bars in the Top Left corner of the app, which displays the following;

At the Top is the user s email. From this Side Menu we only look at **1A Business Info and Year, 1B Set Recording Date,** plus **1C Add Modify Item** in the next Chapter.

2.3   Main Menu

This is the top set of **icons and buttons** leading to the 8 modules in the App. Below is an illustration;

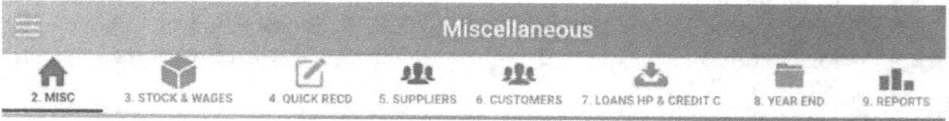

This fits properly on Tablets but only fully accessed on smart phones by **scrolling** side to side. We have a brief look at modules with features covered on this "Accounts in 1 Day".

2.4   Miscellaneous

This is where we land after initial installation and whenever we sign in, every 15 hours. It is a big mixture of facilities and below is an illustration of all the buttons;

On this training we look and utilise the **Dashboard, Cash Register, forms 2B, 2C, 2D, 2E, 2F,** plus **Transaction Edit** at the bottom.

We use only 12 accounts out of the 2500.

2.5   Stock and Wages

This module hosts buttons leading to all facilities to do with Stock and Wages. Below is an illustration of the buttons;

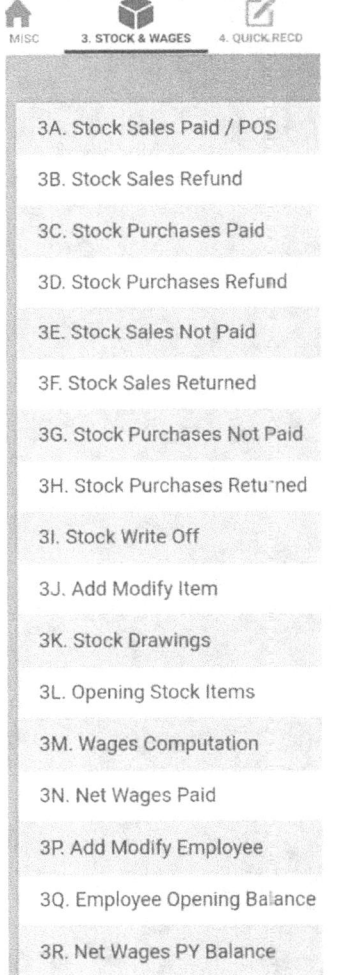

In this "Accounts in 1 Day" we look at **3A for Stock Sales** and **3C Stock Purchases.**

2.6   Loans, HP and Credit Card

This module hosts buttons leading to all facilities to do with Loans, Hire Purchase, and Credit Cards. Below is an illustration of the buttons;

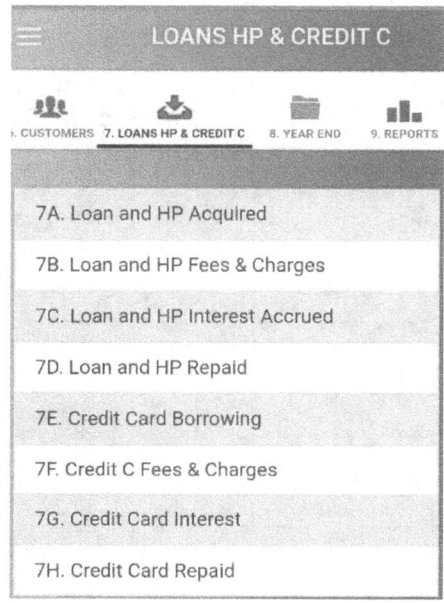

In this "Accounts in 1 Day" we look at only form **7A** for recording a **Borrowed Loan.**

2.7   Period Reports

We have a single Reports button leading to the 3 categories of reports and the Annual General Ledger illustrated below;

Tap to get to a particular category of reports.
The App has **23 reports** in the Period Reports section. Below is an illustration of some of the buttons;

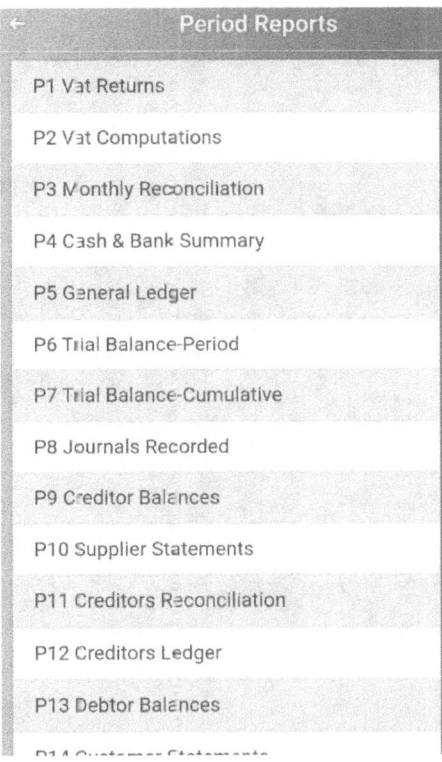

However, this display only shows 13. In this "Accounts in 1 Day" we don't look at any. They are covered in modules 2 and 3 on Sole Trader Bookkeeping.

2.8   Stock Reports

The App has **13 reports** in the Stock Reports section. Below is an illustration of the buttons;

Stock Reports
ST1 Stock Information
ST2 Daily Stock Sales
ST3 Stock Sales By Item
ST4 Monthly Stock Sales & Profit
ST5 Stock Movement
ST6 Monthly Stock Ledger
ST7 Daily Stock Purchases
ST8 Stock Purchases By Item
ST9 Commulative Stock Bought
ST10 Stock Bought & Average Costs
ST11 Annual Stock Sales & Profit
ST12 Annual Stock Ledger
ST13 Stock Taking List

In this "Accounts in 1 Day" we look at **ST1 Stock Information, ST5 Stock Movement, ST11 Stock Sales & Profit,** plus **ST13 Stock Taking List.** The rest are covered in modules 2 and 3 on Sole Trader Bookkeeping.

2.9   Year End Reports

The App automates **80 Year End Reports**. A small business needs very
few. Below is an illustration of buttons leading to a few;

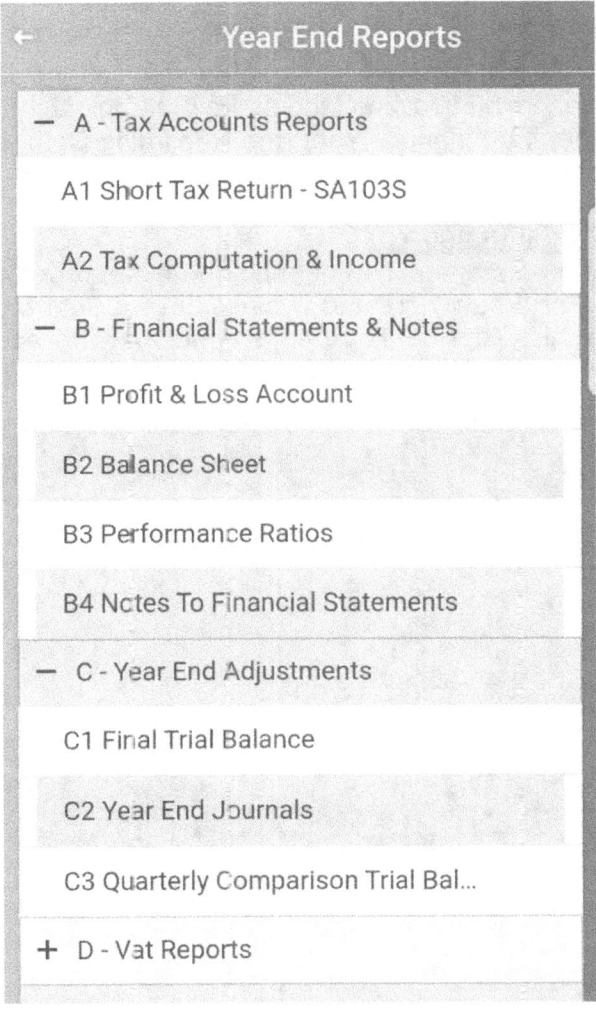

In this "Accounts in 1 Day" we look at **C1 Final Trial Balance, B4 Notes
to Financial Statements**, **B1 Profit and Loss account, B2 Balance
Sheet,** and **A1 Short Tax Return.** The rest are covered in modules 2
and 4 on Sole Trader Accounting.

The rest of the features and facilities are looked at in the second, third
and 4th training modules.
Therefore, if you find a form preceded with a **2**, it implies it's found in
Module 2. If it's preceded with a **7** then it's found in **Module 7**.

Chapter 3. <u>SETTINGS</u>

3.1　　Introduction

The App has several settings which can be modified including the Rate of Tax. However, in this Training Module we only look at the setting of the Business Name, the Financial Year, the Recording Date, plus adding a few item names.

3.2　　Business Info and Year

This is what appears at the Top of each and every report generated by the software. For a newly created business this is light blue and blank. To customise this, Tap the Top Left **3 white bars** to access the side Menu, then select **1A Business Info and Year**, to display the following;

The Top light blue box requires the business name. Just tap the dashes to type in the business name. Some extra Information can be added like the address and Telephone number. There should be a limit of about 85 characters. It can't **update** if it's blank. For this Demo type in **TINY SHOP**.

Different businesses have different financial years especially the Limited Companies. However, many small businesses follow the calendar Year. So this form comes with January as the Set start of the Financial Year, ending in December. However, the Financial Year is modified by tapping the January. From the displayed calendar, select the starting month and Year, then Tap the **Set** button for it to Close. This automates the list of months below, from month 1 to month 12. This setting determines which transactions are included in different monthly and quarterly Reports, basing on the selected Date on the recording form.

Please remember that Financial Accounts is historical, so please change the year accordingly. For this Demo, change the year to 2017. Tap the Update button to Save. If you implement the above guide onto your device, it should look as illustrated below;

3.3   Set Recording Date
The software is set to generate the current calendar date onto each and every recording form opened. However, this can be changed to any other date of preference.

If the recording of transactions is Not daily, following the calendar date, Save time by setting the Recording Date for most of the documents. Since most documents for this Demo business are dated **30th December**, that is the recording date to set.

Tap the Top Left 3 white bars to access the side Menu, then select "**1B Set Recording Date**", to display the following;

Tap the Date which displays a selection calendar. Can change the year or Month, and the specific steps depend on the Android version. For the Demo business let's select **30th December** since most documents require that. And Tap the year to change it to 2017, then the "**Set**" button. Then **Update**, and all recording forms open with the set date. After updating, it's also possible to **revert back** by tapping the Lower button "**Set Back To Current Date**".

3.4   Adding Stock Items
The illustration of the recording of Income and Cost of Sales is focused on documents with Stock items. So we start by adding individual stock item accounts.

The software is designed with 1500 accounts to cater for different Stock items starting at number 1201. However, it's only the allocated accounts which are displayed.

In Settings Menu, Tap button **"1C Add Modify Item"** to access the following;

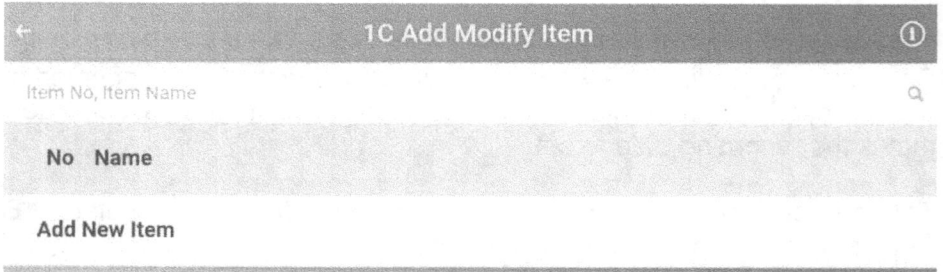

Tap the "**Add New Item**" to expose the following;

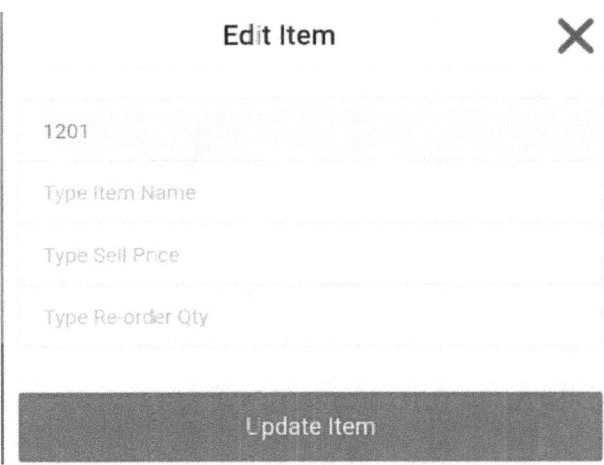

This 1201 account is customized by allocating it to the named item of Stock or Service. Type the **item Name, Selling Price, and the Re-order Quantity**, then Update the item. Let's set the Re-order Quantity for each item at **5 units**, and get the rest of the information from the Sales document illustrated below;

TINY SHOP			3
Cash Sales RECEIPT			
	Date:	30-Dec	
Items	**Price**	**QTY**	**Net Cost**
Sony	321.20	18	5,781.60
Nokia	543.40	24	13,041.60
Iphone	386.10	17	6,563.70
Galaxy	272.80	30	8,184.00
3A	Total Amount		33,570.90
Paid by:	Cash		

It saves time to type the sell Price for a particular item **only once**, Not at the time of selling. The **Re-order Quantity** is aimed at providing a **warning whenever the Stock level is low**, for a new stock purchase to be done in time.

The procedure is Tapping "**Add New Item**", typing the item Name, the Sell Price, and Re-order quantity before updating. Once that is done for the 4 items, the list looks as illustrated below;

← 1C Add Modify Item

Item No, Item Name

No   Name

Add New Item

1201 Sony **Sell Price:** 321.2 **Re-Order Qty:** 5

1202 Nokia **Sell Price:** 543.4 **Re-Order Qty:** 5

1203 Iphone **Sell Price:** 386.1 **Re-Order Qty:** 5

1204 Galaxy **Sell Price:** 272.8 **Re-Order Qty:** 5

After adding items in the software, a Record is started about each one. Against each one, we can record a Purchase, a Sale, a Write off, etc. Without any activity, we can extract some information about them, found on **Report ST1**. This is accessed in the **Reports Module 9**, **select Stock Reports and Tap the Top one**. If the four above items are Set Up in the software, the ST1 Report should be as illustrated below;

	Stock Information					ST1	
#	Item	Stock Bal	Re-Order Qty	Avg Cost	Sell Price	Unit Profit	Profit %
1	Sony	0	5		321.20		%
2	Nokia	0	5		543.40		%
3	Iphone	0	5		386.10		%
4	Galaxy	0	5		272.80		%

This report shows that we have four items recorded, with their selling Price and Re-order quantity. The Re-order Quantity box turns Red whenever the Stock Balance is less than the Re-order Quantity. The rest of the boxes are blank.

Chapter 4. <u>CASH CAPITAL</u>

4.1 Introduction

All businesses start with **Capital**, which is money Invested by the business **Owner**. In principal this money **crosses** from the owner into the business. It's received by the business in either cash, cheque, electronically, or straight onto a bank account. Below is a document which was prepared to acknowledge **Receipt** of the money, and we use to illustrate the recording;

Tiny Shop	①
Receipt **Date:**	01-Dec
For: **Owner's Investment**	
2E	**Amount** 19,000.00
Rcvd by: Cash	

4.2 Recording Money Capital

Use **form 2E in Module "2 MISC"**. Tap the button "**2E Money Capital Invested**" to get the following display;

Money Capital Invested							ⓘ
Date	Account	Amount	Narration	Doc No.	F Mth	F Qua	
30/12/2018 ▾	To	Bank1 (205) ▾		Money Capital	1	12	4th Q1
30/12/2018 ▾	From	Capital Add (271) ▾		Money Capital	1	12	4th Q1

What to record on the form is copied from the source document above. Tap the **calendar dropdown** to change the Date to 1st December. Tap the dropdown by **"Bank 1 (205)"** to change the account "**To**" Cash 212 which received the money. The account "**From**" should be Capital Added 271 which is **pre-selected**.

Type 19,000 into the Top amount box, and the **Credit amount is automated** below. The default narration can be modified by **overtyping** to "Cash Capital".

The document number is **automated to 1** since it's the very first document to be recorded. The **Financial Month is automated to 12** basing on the set Financial Year and the Date on the form. The quarter should be ignored, its handled in Module 3. If the above guide is implemented on your device, it should look as illustrated below, before Saving;

Date			Account		Amount	Narration	Doc No.	F Mth
			Money Capital Invested					ⓘ
01/12/2018 ▾	To		Cash	(212) ▾	19000.00	Cash Capital	1	12
01/12/2018 ▾	From		Capital Add (271) ▾		-19000.00	Cash Capital	1	12

Then Tap in a blank space on the device to expose the bottom buttons. Tap the **Save and Close button**, or Close if not required. The **major task with this recording** was selecting the correct Top account "**To**", and that is not difficult.

4.3   Trace Cash Capital on Accounts

The Bookkeeping procedure is **copying** information from documents, recording onto accounts located centrally in a **Ledger Book**, and in software it's presented as a **Ledger report**. The Ledger Book or report normally has many accounts with many transactions. So it's summarized into a **Trial Balance**.

All recorded transactions end up on Accounts, which are presented as a **Ledger report**. This Report shows **Accounts** with details of individual transactions recorded onto them. Both **Received** (Debit) and **Given** (Credit) values are recorded in the same column since mobile devices are small. It shows records made to all accounts for the business.

To access this report scroll to the **Right**, tap "**9 Reports**", then "**Annual General Ledger**". This one shows all documents and transactions recorded for the whole year, it doesn't classify according to month or quarter. If you record the above document onto your device, the Ledger should look as illustrated below;

TINY SHOP					
Jan-2017 to Dec-2017					
	Annual General Ledger		To Trial Balance		
Dates	Narrations		Doc No	Trans No	Amount
212 Cash					
1-12-17	Cash Capital		1	1	19,000.00
212 Cash Balance					19,000.00
271 Capital Added					
1-12-17	Cash Capital		1	1	-19,000.00
271 Capital Added Balance					-19,000.00

This is the recorded Cash Capital in the Ledger. We see the 19,000 recorded as **Received (To)** on the Cash account, as a positive without a sign. And it's also recorded as **Given (From)** away by the Capital account, as a negative. The Capital account is where we record values coming **from the owner**, into the business. The Debit and Credit concepts are introduced later.

There is a **Balance** at the bottom of each account, which is calculated by deducting what is given from what is received. The balance on each of the accounts is equal to the single entry made so far. The **Cash balance** available to spend by the business **increases** from Zero to 19,000. The money owed by the business to the owner, on account 271, increases by the amount Invested.

4.4   Error Correction

Any error on the above transaction is **corrected by tapping the <u>blue transaction number</u>**, which opens up to the original recording form for any modification.

Transaction Edit
This is the last button at the bottom of module **2 MISC,** illustrated here. When tapped it gives access to the list of transactions recorded in the software. It also provides an opportunity to **Correct or Edit** a recording, plus the chance to **delete unwanted transactions.**

There is a **Green Edit** and **Red Delete** buttons on the bottom extreme Right of each recorded transaction. Tap either of the 2 for action.

4.5   Cash Capital on Summary Trial Balance

A Trial Balance is a report prepared to **confirm the accuracy of Double Entry and the absence of balancing errors**.

One of the Accounting regulations is **Double Entry**, the recording of every value on **2 accounts**, once on the **Giving account** and once on the **Receiving account**. If this is violated then it's exposed by the Trial Balance for correction.

There is also a requirement to balance each and every account, by deducting what was **Given** from what was **Received**. If there is an **error in the balancing process**, it's also exposed by the Trial Balance for correction.

However, the possibility of these errors in this software is very remote due to automation. So the Trial Balance is used more as a **Summary of the Ledger**, showing the balances on each of the **accounts**. The above General Ledger report in the software has a **direct access button** at the Top, "**To Trial Balance**". When tapped, the following is seen;

TINY SHOP	
Jan-2017 to Dec-2017	
ANNUAL TRIAL BALANCE	**ATB**
To Quarterly TB	**FINAL BALANCES**
212 Cash	19,000.00
271 Capital Added	-19,000.00
Difference To Investigate	**0.00**

This is an Annual Trial Balance since its not based on months or quarters but shows balances on all accounts from the very beginning to the end of the year. Period Reports are avoided in this module. The above Ledger report with it's 2 accounts is summarized by listing the only 2 balances on the accounts. And the negative balance is deducted from the positive balance to get a **Zero difference** at the bottom. Which confirms that every value was recorded on 2 accounts, and that each account was balanced properly. If you recall we selected 2 accounts on the recording form, and the **balancing is automatically** done by the software.

By set up on the recording forms, we don't expect to find a Trial Balance difference since the **corresponding figures are automated**. The common error could be selecting the wrong accounts, but Not a difference in amounts.

5.1   Introduction

Our demonstration business is a TINY SHOP which buys in Stock before it's sold for a Profit. Below is a Stock Purchases receipt to illustrate the recording;

FUN Mobiles			②
RECEIPT	**To: Tiny Shop**		
	Stock	Date:	30-Dec
Items	**Price**	**QTY**	**Net Cost**
Sony	125.00	25	3,125.00
Nokia	309.00	25	7,725.00
Iphone	147.00	25	3,675.00
Galaxy	38.00	30	2,640.00
3C	**Total Amount**		17,165.00
Paid by:	Cash		

5.2   Recording

The App has separate forms for Cash and Credit Stock Purchases. The form for this Cash Purchase is found in **Module 3 for Stock and Wages**. Tap on **3C Stock Purchases Paid** to access the following form;

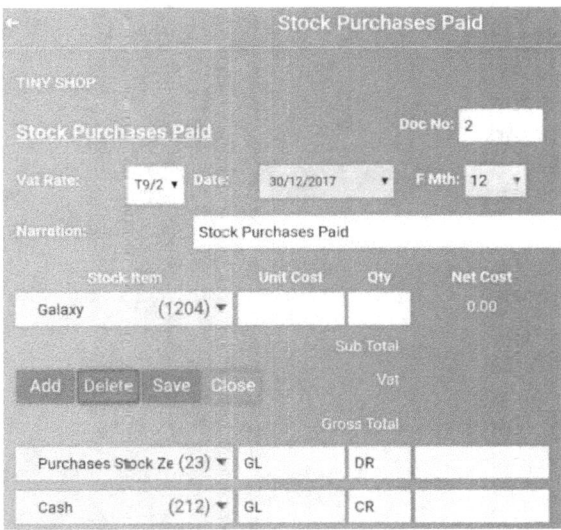

Although this form comes with some information, it should be edited to exactly match what is on the Stock Purchase Receipt. It comes with an **editable date** and Financial Month 12, based on the Financial Year set earlier. The default narration can be modified by overtyping. The editable document number is automated to 2, since it's the second one to be recorded.

It comes with one Stock item, which is at the Top of the alphabetic listing, and it may come with an average Cost Price if there is any previously recorded purchase. Tap the drop down to select the appropriate Stock item. Can type its **identity number or Name** in the dropdown of the search box to quickly select from a long list. Change the Unit Cost if different from what is displayed, and type the number of units bought. PLEASE NOTE, **we record the number of individual units, not dozens or boxes. Unless the items are also sold in dozens or boxes.**

Adding the quantity gives an **automated Net Cost** computed by multiplying the Cost Price with Quantity. To get more rows for Stock items, Tap the **Add Button**, and if they are too many, tap the **Delete Button**. For each item, confirm the Net Cost agrees with the source document, or should **verify the subtotal agrees** before saving. Any error should be corrected at this stage.

Below are the two **Ledger accounts**. The default Purchases account to **Debit** is number 23 which can be changed using the drop down. Since we aim to have all Purchases for this Demo on **account 25,** it should be selected. The default Paying account to **Credit** is the Cash account, which can also be changed using the drop down. The amounts on the right are automated **from the Gross Total above.**

Then Tap on the device to expose the bottom buttons. Tap the **Save Button** to store what is recorded. If it's Not required then just Tap **Close**.

On the right is an illustration of the filled form just before Saving;

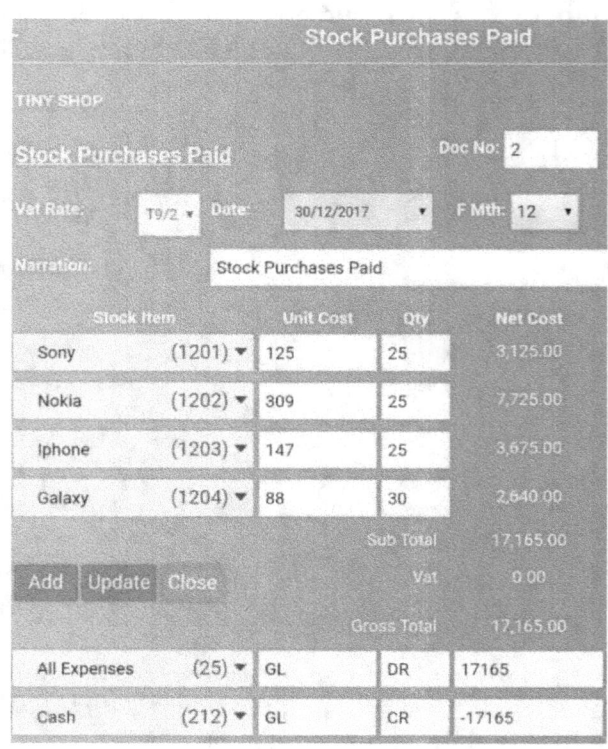

Stock Purchases Paid

TINY SHOP

Stock Purchases Paid

Doc No: 2

Vat Rate: T9/2 ▾ Date: 30/12/2017 ▾ F Mth: 12 ▾

Narration: Stock Purchases Paid

Stock Item		Unit Cost	Qty	Net Cost
Sony	(1201) ▾	125	25	3,125.00
Nokia	(1202) ▾	309	25	7,725.00
Iphone	(1203) ▾	147	25	3,675.00
Galaxy	(1204) ▾	88	30	2,640.00
			Sub Total	17,165.00

Add Update Close

			Vat	0.00
			Gross Total	17,165.00
All Expenses	(25) ▾	GL	DR	17165
Cash	(212) ▾	GL	CR	-17165

Then Tap in a blank space on the device to expose the bottom buttons. Tap the **Save and Close button** at the bottom, or Close if not required. What makes this **very simple**, provided the correct form is selected, even if account 23 isn't changed to 25, it **doesn't change the Profit or Balance Sheet.**

5.3   Trace Stock Purchases on Accounts

This is a Cummulative Ledger since it shows previously recorded documents. Please Note, that the Account To is always at the **Top**, and Account From is normally **below**, unless stated otherwise.

What was recorded using form 3C was saved on the selected accounts 25 and 212. This is seen when the General Ledger report is displayed. To access this report scroll to the **Right**, tap "**9 Reports**", then "**Annual General Ledger**". After recording documents 1 and 2, the General Ledger should look as illustrated below;

;

TINY SHOP					
Jan-2017 to Dec-2017					
Annual General Ledger			To Trial Balance		
Dates	Narrations		Doc No	Trans No	Amount
25 All Expenses					
30-12-17	Stock Purchases Paid		2	2	17,165.00
25 All Expenses Balance					17,165.00
212 Cash					
1-12-17	Cash Capital		1	1	19,000.00
30-12-17	Stock Purchases Paid		2	2	-17,165.00
212 Cash Balance					1,835.00
271 Capital Added					
1-12-17	Cash Capital		1	1	-19,000.00
271 Capital Added Balance					-19,000.00

This report shows the **2 entries** for each and every transaction/ value recorded. Transaction 1 is the Capital Invested of 19,000. Transaction 2 is the Stock Purchases of **17,165** Given To account 25, From account 212. When balanced, we see the Cash balance reduced from 19,000 to **1,835**, while the All Expenses balance rose to **17,165.**

5.4   Stock Purchases on Summary Trial Balance

This is a Cummulative Trial Balance since it shows previously recorded documents. The balance on each account in the Ledger is copied to generate the Summary Trial Balance. This Trial Balance can be accessed without going via the Annual General Ledger. To access this report scroll to the **Right**, tap "**9 Reports**", then "**Annual Trial Balance**". When tapped, the following is seen;

TINY SHOP	
Jan-2017 to Dec-2017	
ANNUAL TRIAL BALANCE	**ATB**
To Quarterly TB	**FINAL BALANCES**
25 All Expenses	17,165.00
212 Cash	1,835.00
271 Capital Added	-19,000.00
Difference To Investigate	**0.00**

The **17,165** is seen against **account 25,** while the corresponding entry is part of the balance on **account 212,** as seen on the ledger account above. Using a calculator we can confirm if the total Positives equate to the Total Negative of 19,000.

Chapter 6. <u>POINT OF SALE</u>

6.1 Introduction

Some businesses buy and sell Stock items, while others deal in services. Instead of simply recording the Income value, we can record the quantity of Sold items, which initiates the **auto and continuous Stock Taking exercise**. However, for this to be effective, all transactions involving Stock must be recorded, all the way from Opening Stock, Purchases and Sales, Returns and Refunds, plus Stock written off. The App has separate forms for Cash and Credit Sales.

6.2 Point of Sale

This is a software facility used to **record a Paid Sale, Calculate Change, and Print a Receipt.** It's also known as a Point of Purchase since it's where the buyer pays for their Purchase Below is a Cash Sales Receipt to illustrate the functionality of the Point of Sale feature;

TINY SHOP ③			
Cash Sales RECEIPT			
Date:	30-Dec		
Items	**Price**	**QTY**	**Net Cost**
Sony	321.20	18	5,781.60
Nokia	543.40	24	13,041.60
Iphone	386.10	17	6,563.70
Galaxy	272.80	30	8,184.00
3A	Total Amount		33,570.90
Paid by:	Cash		

The Point of Sale facility is part of Form 3A found in **section 3 for Stock and Wages,** illustrated here;

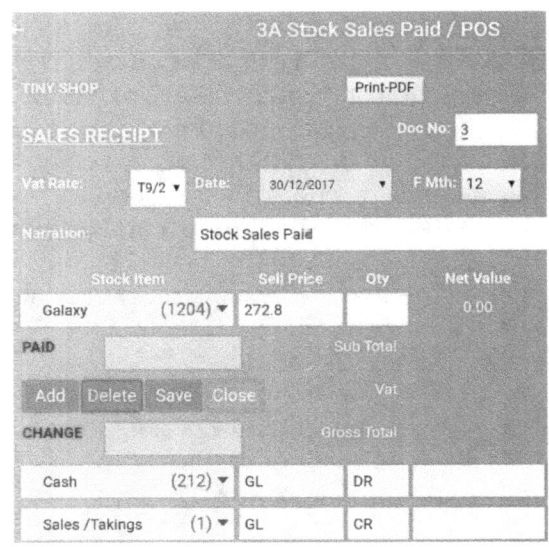

6.3   Recording Paid Sale

The initial function of this form is recording the Paid Stock Sale. It opens with some information to save time. In a selling environment it's the verbal and physical information fed to a Cashier that is typed instantly. There is No other source document and that's why it has a provision for being **Printed**, to get a buyer's and seller's copy.

The form opens with an **editable date** and Financial Month 12, based on the Financial Year set earlier. The default narration can be modified by overtyping. The editable document number is automated to 3, since it's the third to be recorded.

It comes with one Stock item, which is at the Top of the alphabetic listing, together with its **Selling Price** set earlier to **save time**. Tap the drop down to select the appropriate Stock item. Can type its **identity number or Name** in the dropdown search box to quickly select from a long list. The selling Price can only be modified by tapping the Add Modify button on the items list.

PLEASE NOTE, **the unit item for Sale should be uniform with Purchases and write offs. We can't mix boxes or dozens with units, otherwise the records become meaningless.**

Add the quantity to get the **Net Value automated** by multiplying the Sell Price with Quantity. To get more rows for Stock items, Tap the **Add Button**, and if they are too many, tap the **Delete Button**. For training purposes we confirm the Net Value for each item agrees with the source document, or we should verify the **subtotal agrees** before saving. Any error should be corrected at this stage.

Below are the two **Ledger accounts**. The default **Receiving** account to **Debit** is the Cash account, which can be changed using the drop down. The default Income account to Credit is Sales which can be changed using the drop down. Since we are using only **account 5 for All Income**, this should be changed to account 5. The amounts on the right are **automated from the Gross Total above**.

Without the need to calculate Change, the Sale information on the form is ready to Save. Please Note that the **Pink Change Calculating Boxes** are blank, as illustrated below;

Just like the previous recording forms, if the Save button is hit then information is **recorded** on each of the **Ledger accounts**, plus each of the **Stock item accounts**.

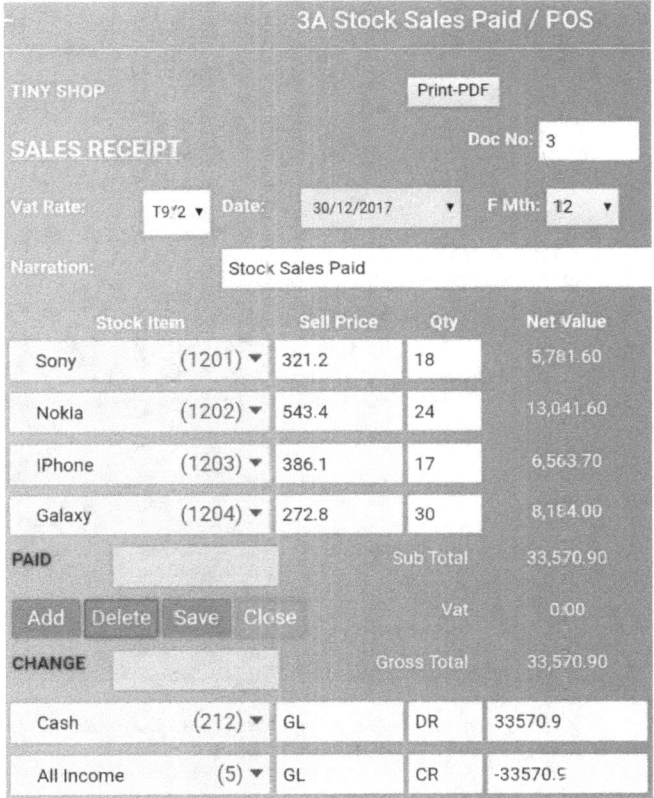

6.4   Change Calculation

This form is equipped with the ability to **calculate Change**, saving the need for a calculator or wrong mental calculation. Change calculation is **necessary** when the buyer pays more than the required amount to pay for the items. This process is initiated when the Paid amount is typed into the **PAID Box.** The Change amount is instantly displayed in the **CHANGE Box** below the Save button, as illustrated below;

The Change is calculated as the **difference** between the amount Paid and the Gross Total for sold items. Below is an illustration of the form showing the **paid amount of 33,600**, and **the calculated change of 29.10** just before Saving;

3A Stock Sales Paid / POS			
TINY SHOP		Print-PDF	
SALES RECEIPT		Doc No: 3	
Vat Rate: T9/2 ▼	Date: 30/12/2017 ▼	F Mth: 12 ▼	
Narration:	Stock Sales Paid		

Stock Item		Sell Price	Qty	Net Value
Sony	(1201) ▼	321.2	18	5,781.60
Nokia	(1202) ▼	543.4	24	13,041.60
IPhone	(1203) ▼	386.1	17	6,563.70
Galaxy	(1204) ▼	272.8	30	8,184.00
PAID	33600	33600	Sub Total	33,570.90
Add Delete Save Close			Vat	0.00
CHANGE	29.10	29.10	Gross Total	33,570.90
Cash	(212) ▼ GL	DR	33570.9	
All Income	(5) ▼ GL	CR	-33570.9	

6.5   Receipt Printing

It's mentioned earlier that there is no other source document for this recording apart from the verbal and physical information of what is being sold or bought. In addition to the **Recording and Change Calculation features**, this form is **Printed** to provide **evidence** the Sale took place, and money was Received for the Sale. It's printed as a **Receipt** and the copy given to the buyer is the **source document** for recording in their Records. On the **seller's side,** the printed retained copy supports the recorded Sale on the accounts. But for this software, it's **not** a source document since the record was based on verbal and physical information.

Tapping the Save button closes the form. So it's best that printing is done **before saving**. Printing is done by Tapping the Print-PDF button, which leads to a Print Preview screen, where we either select the PDF creation option or the connected Mobile Printer. Much as the Printing procedure is not complicated, we look at it properly in Module 2, Small Business Accounts.

If a PDF is created from the above Sales Receipt, it looks as illustrated below;

```
TINY SHOP
                                              Doc No:3
SALES RECEIPT

Vat Rate:              Date:    Dec 30, 2017      F Mth:12
Narration:             Stock Sales Paid

            Stock Item      Sell Price    Qty    Net Value
            1201 - Sony        321.2       18     5,781.60
            1202 - Nokia       543.4       24    13,041.60
            1203 - Phone       386.1       17     6,563.70
            1204 - Galaxy      272.8       30     8,184.00
PAID                              Sub Total      33,570.90
33600
                                      Vat           0.00
CHANGE                         Gross Total      33,570.90
29.10
```

To finalise the most important recording function of form 3A, the information entered must be saved. Tap the **Save Button** to store what is recorded. If it's not required then Tap **Close**.

What makes this **very simple**, provided the correct form is selected, even if account 1 isn't changed to 5, this **doesn't change the Profit or Balance Sheet figures.**

6.6   Trace Stock Sales on Accounts

This is a Cummulative Ledger since it shows previously recorded documents. All recorded documents end up on Ledger accounts. To access this report scroll to the **Right**, tap "**9 Reports**", then "**Annual General Ledger**". Below is an illustration of the Cummulative Ledger, with all documents from number 1;

The Sales value of 33,570.90 is seen coming **From account 5** as a **negative**, and increases it's negative balance from Zero. The same value is seen **Going To** the Cash account as a **positive**, and it's balance rises to 35,405.90

TINY SHOP				
Jan-2017 to Dec-2017				
Annual General Ledger		To Trial Balance		
Dates	Narrations	Doc No	Trans No	Amount
5 All Income				
30-12-17	Stock Sales Paid	3	3	-33,570.90
5 All Income Balance				-33,570.90
25 All Expenses				
30-12-17	Stock Purchases Paid	2	2	17,165.00
25 All Expenses Balance				17,165.00
212 Cash				
1-12-17	Cash Capital	1	1	19,000.00
30-12-17	Stock Purchases Paid	2	2	-17,165.00
30-12-17	Stock Sales Paid	3	3	33,570.90
212 Cash Balance				35,405.90
271 Capital Added				
1-12-17	Cash Capital	1	1	-19,000.00
271 Capital Added Balance				-19,000.00

6.7   Stock Sales on Summary Trial Balance

This is a Cummulative Trial Balance since it shows previously recorded documents. The balance on each account in the Ledger is copied to generate the Summary Trial Balance below, after recording Stock Sales;

TINY SHOP	
Jan-2017 to Dec-2017	
ANNUAL TRIAL BALANCE	ATB
To Quarterly TB	FINAL BALANCES
5 All Income	-33,570.90
25 All Expenses	17,165.00
212 Cash	35,405.90
271 Capital Added	-19,000.00
Difference To Investigate	**0.00**

These balances are extracted from the above Ledger, and all figures do agree with what is on the accounts. The **33,570.90** is seen against **account 5,** while the corresponding entry is part of the balance on **account 212,** as seen on the Ledger account above. Using a calculator, we can confirm if the total Positives equate to the Total Negatives, to generate a Zero difference.

Chapter 7. <u>STOCK REPORTS</u>

The software generates upto 13 Stock Reports but we look at only 4 on this 1 Day Module. Anc these reports are accessed by simply touching a button.

7.1   Stock Information

This is a Summary report which provides information about the items and services sold by a business, and alerts when an item is due for **re-stocking**. Below is an illustration for the Demo business;

TINY SHOP

Jan-2017 to Dec-2017

			Stock Information				ST1	
#	Item	Stock Bal	Re-Order Qty	Avg Cost	Sell Price	Unit Profit	Profit %
1	Sony	7	5	125.00	321.20	196.20	156.96%
2	Nokia	1		309.00	543.40	234.40	75.86%
3	Iphone	8	5	147.00	386.10	239.10	162.65%
4	Galaxy	0		88.00	272.30	184.80	210.00%

It shows the item Name, Stock Balance, Re-order Quantity, Average Cost, Selling Price, Unit Profit, plus the Percent Profit generated on each Item.

The **Stock Balance** is derived by adding the Opening Stock to Purchased Stock, and deducting the Sold Units, all the way from the start of the Year. However, Returns and Write Offs are also considered. The detail of this is found on the **ST5** Stock Movement Report.

The **Re-order Quantity** and **Selling Price** are recorded when registering the Item, and can be edited ary time. The **Average Cost** is derived by dividing the Total Cost of Opening and Net bought items, by the number of Cummulative Units. The detail of this is found on Report **ST10**.

The **Unit Profit** is derived by deducting the Average Cost from Selling Price. The **Profit Percent** is cerived by dividing the Unit Profit by the Average Cost.

There is an **Alert if the Stock Balance is less than the Re-order Quantity,** reminding the business to re-stock. If the alert comes on, the

Re-order Quantity changes colour from **Black to YELLOW**, and the box is coloured **RED**. However, this alert should be ignored in case of service items. The above report has a **re-order alert** for Nokia and Galaxy.

7.2   Stock Movement

This report provides a general overview of Stock activity from start to the **Year to Date, or Year End**. Below is an illustration for Tiny Shop;

TINY SHOP					
Jan-2017 to Dec-2017					
		Stock Movement			ST5
#	Item	Opening Balance	Qty Bought	Total Sold	Stock Balance
1	Sony	0	25	-18	7
2	Nokia	0	25	-24	1
3	Iphone	0	25	-17	8
4	Galaxy	0	30	-30	0
	Totals	0	105	-89	16

It shows the Opening Balance, Total Quantity Bought, Total Quantity Sold, and the Stock Balance for each and every item stocked by the business.

The **Opening Balance** are quantities brought forward from the previous Financial Year. The **Quantity Bought** is generated by adding figures from the Cash and Credit Purchases forms, and deducting the Refunded, Returned, and written off items.

The **Quantity Sold** is generated by adding figures from the Cash and Credit Sales forms, and deducting the Refunded and Returned items. The Quantity Bought and Sold stretches from Month 1 to either the Year to Date or the Year End. And they are both **Net figures**, after deductions.

The **Stock Balance** is computed by adding the Net Quantity Bought to Opening Balance, and deducting the Net Quantity Sold. We also have Totals at the bottom of each column.

7.3   Annual Stock Sales & Profit

This a summary report which shows Annual Sales and Gross Profit. For each product it shows the **Average Cost, Quantity Sold, Total Cost, Sales Value,** plus **Gross Profit.** Below is an illustration for Tiny Shop;

TINY SHOP

Jan-2017 to Dec-2017

	Annual Stock Sales & Profit				ST11
Item	Average Cost	Qty Sold	Total Cost	Sales Value	Gross Profit
Sony	125.00	18	2,250.00	5,781.60	3,531.60
Nokia	309.00	24	7,416.00	13,041.60	5,625.60
Iphone	147.00	17	2,499.00	6,563.70	4,064.70
Galaxy	88.00	30	2,640.00	8,184.00	5,544.00
Total		89	14,805.00	33,570.90	18,765.90

The **Average Cost** is derived by dividing the **Total Cost** of Opening and Net Purchased Items To Date, by the Opening and **Net Quantity** bought To Date. The **Quantity sold** is generated by adding figures from the Cash and Credit Sales forms, and deducting the Refunded and Returned items.

The **Total Cost of what was Sold**, is computed by multiplying the Average Cost with the Quantity Sold. The **Sales Value** is generated by adding figures from the Cash and Credit Sales forms, and deducting the Refunded and Returned items. The **Gross Profit** is computed by deducting the Total Cost from the Sales Value for each item. And we have Annual Totals at the bottom of each column.

Using a calculator, we can confirm the figures since the formulas are provided.

7.4   Stock Taking List

This report provides the quantities of unsold stock items, which are multiplied with the average cost to get the **Closing Stock Figure** for the Balance Sheet at the Year End, or at any time. Below is an illustration for the Demo business;

TINY SHOP

Jan-2017 to Dec-2017

	Stock Taking List			ST13
#	Item	Average Cost	Stock Balance	Closing Value
1	Sony	125	7	875.00
2	Nokia	309	1	309.00
3	Iphone	147	8	1,176.00
	Totals		16	2,360.00

The **Stock Balance** is computed by adding the Net Quantity Bought to Opening Balance, and deducting the Net Quantity Sold, as illustrated by ST5. The **Closing Value** is computed by multiplying the Stock Balance with the **Average Cost** per unit. We also have Totals at the bottom of each column. However, in this module we don't need the closing stock figure since we don't record year-end adjustments.

Chapter 8. <u>CASH DEPOSIT</u>

Page

8.1 Introduction

This is the taking of liquid Cash from the business, **to a Bank for safe custody.** It's either taken straight to the Bank Cashier or a form is initially filled in. Below is a Demo Deposit Slip;

Natwest Bank		
	Deposit Slip No: 56	④
Date: 30-Dec		
2C	**Cash Total**	29,200.00

8.2 Recording

As indicated, a Deposit is recorded using form 2C, illustrated below;

Bank Deposit, Withdraw & Transfers							①

Date			Account	Amount	Narration	Doc No.	F Mth	F
30/12/2017 ▼	To	Cash	(212) ▼			4	12	4t
30/12/2017 ▼	From	Bank1	(205) ▼			4	12	4t

This form comes with some information but it should be edited to exactly match what is on the Deposit Slip. It comes with an **editable date** and Financial Month 12, based on the Financial Year set earlier. The **editable document** number is automated to 4, since it's the fourth document to be recorded.

For boxes in the **accounts column**, the money comes "**From**" the Cash account, "**To**" the Bank account. So Tap the Top dropdown to change the account to, to the main **Bank account 205**. And Tap the Lower dropdown to change to the **Cash account 212**, where the money is coming from.

Type the amount of 29,200 in the Top box, which automates the lower amount into a negative. The positive amount is the Debit while the negative amount is the Credit entry.

And finally it's the narration or brief description which should be; **Cash Deposit.** In case you record the above Deposit Slip, before saving, the form should look as illustrated below;

Date			Account		Amount	Narration	Doc No.	F Mth	F Q
30/12/2017	▾	To	Bank1	(205) ▾	29200.00	Cash Deposit	4	12	4th
30/12/2017	▾	From	Cash	(212) ▾	-29200.00	Cash Deposit	4	12	4th

Then Tap in a blank space on the device to expose the bottom buttons. Tap the **Save and Close button** at the bottom, or Close if not required.

The **simplicity** of this task revolves around a specialised form with restricted accounts. We just have to be sure of where the Cash is coming "**From**", and where it's going "**To**", with the **"i"** on the recording form also providing guidance.

8.3   Trace Cash Deposit on Accounts

Like all transactions, a Cash Deposit ends up on 2 accounts in the Ledger. The Cash account where the Cash came from is the Giver and its **balance is reduced** by the 29,200. While the Bank account which received the money, its **balance increases**. Below is an illustration;

Annual General Ledger		To Trial Balance		
Dates	Narrations	Doc No	Trans No	Amount
5 All Income				
30-12-17	Stock Sales Paid	3	3	-33,570.90
5 All Income Balance				-33,570.90
25 All Expenses				
30-12-17	Stock Purchases Paid	2	2	17,165.00
25 All Expenses Balance				**17,165.00**
205 Bank1				
30-12-17	Cash Deposit	4	4	29,200.00
205 Bank1 Balance				**29,200.00**
212 Cash				
1-12-17	Cash Capital	1	1	19,000.00
30-12-17	Stock Purchases Paid	2	2	-17,165.00
30-12-17	Stock Sales Paid	3	3	33,570.90
30-12-17	Cash Deposit	4	4	-29,200.00
212 Cash Balance				**6,205.90**
271 Capital Added				
1-12-17	Cash Capital	1	1	-19,000.00
271 Capital Added Balance				**-19,000.00**

This is the **Annual General Ledger (AGL),** accessed by scrolling to the **Right**, tap "**9 Reports**", and tap the **AGL button**.

The transaction in focus is number 4. The **29,200 Goes (is debited)** To the Bank account and comes From (**credited** to) the Cash account. In case of an error with any of the above transactions, tap the **blue transaction number**, which leads to the original recording form. Make the required correction and Tap the Update button.

8.4   Summary Trial Balance after Deposit

The Cash Deposit is a transfer of value **From** the Cash account **To** the Bank account. The amount is the same for both accounts, although it affects each account in a way that is **opposite** to the other. Below is an illustration of the Summary Trial Balance with changed balances;

TINY SHOP	
Jan-2017 to Dec-2017	
ANNUAL TRIAL BALANCE	**ATB**
To Quarterly TB	**FINAL BALANCES**
5 All Income	-33,570.90
25 All Expenses	17,165.00
205 Bank1	29,200.00
212 Cash	6,205.90
271 Capital Added	-19,000.00
Difference To Investigate	**0.00**

This is the **Annual Trial Balance (ATB),** accessed by scrolling to the **Right**, tap "**9 Reports**", and tap the **ATB button**.

Compared to the Trial Balance just after document 3, the Cash balance has reduced by **29200**, while the Bank account is introduced with an increased balance of the same amount.

Please remember, these balances come from Accounts in the **Ledger**.

Chapter 9. LOAN AND INTEREST

9.1 Introduction

Borrowing money from the Bank or other lenders is common practice in business. The amount borrowed is normally extracted from a Loan Agreement. Below is a Demo to illustrate the recording of a borrowed Loan;

LOAN AGREEMENT	(5)	LN: 743
Borrower: <u>Tiny Shop</u>		**Date:** 01-Dec
	To Bank Account	
Amount: 1,200.00	7A	**Period:** <u>12 Months</u>
31-Dec		
Monthly Interest: 30.00	2F **Monthly Total Repayment:** 130.00	
Total Interest: 360.00	**Repayments Start:**	31-Dec

The recording of a borrowed Loan is different from the recording of monthly interest, and is different from the recording of Monthly repayments.

9.2 Recording A Loan

This involves the recording of only the amount borrowed, also known as the **Principal Loan**. As per guide, the form to use is **7A**, Tap the **Loan and HP Acquired** button to reveal the following form;

	7A Loan and HP Acquired						ⓘ
Date		Account	Amount	Narration	Doc No.	F Mth	F Q
30/12/2017 ▾	To	Bank1 (205) ▾		Loan / HP Acquired	5	12	4th
30/12/2017 ▾	From	Hire Purcha (230) ▾		Loan / HP Acquired	5	12	4th

This form comes with some information but it should be edited to exactly match what is on the Loan Agreement. It comes with an **editable date** and Financial Month 12, based on the Financial Year set earlier. Tap the Date box to change to 1st December. The **editable document** number is automated to 5, since it's the 5th document to be recorded.

For boxes in the **accounts column**, the money comes "**From**" the Loan account, "**To**" the Bank account 205, which is **pre-selected**. Tap the

Lower dropdown to change to the Loan1 account 225, where the money is coming **from**. Please Note, the dropdown shows 5 Loan accounts, plus others.

Type the Loan amount of 1,200 in the Top box, which automates the lower amount into a negative. The positive amount is the Debit while the negative amount is the Credit entry.

Modify the narration or brief description to **Loan Acquired,** by deleting "/HP". In case you record this Loan on your device, before Saving, the form should look as illustrated below;

Date			Account		Amount	Narration	Doc No.	F Mth	F (
01/12/2017	▾	To	Bank1	(205) ▾	1200.00	Loan	5	12	4th
01/12/2017	▾	From	Loan1	(225) ▾	-1200.00	Loan	5	12	4th

Loan and HP Acquired ⓘ

Then Tap in a blank space on the device to expose the bottom buttons. Tap the **Save and Close button**, or Close if not required. The **simplicity** of this task is that the only challenge was selecting the account From. The rest are straight forward.

9.3   Recording Interest

On a few occasions a Loan is acquired without Interest and that is often on a personal basis. However, interest is chargeable on most Loans and it's often added on a monthly basis. It becomes due at the every end of month and that is when it's recorded. If the Loan is paid off earlier, then the monthly interest also stops earlier.

Loan Interest is an expense to the business and in this 1 Day Accounts format we endeavour to record **All Expenses** on account 5, as mentioned earlier. Although the specifically designed form for recording Loan Interest is 7C, **we instead use 2F** for simplicity. The above Loan Agreement has a monthly interest of 30, which accrues or becomes an expense at the end of each Month. So we use the last day of the Month to record. Tap the **2F** button to expose the following;

Date		JN		Account		Amount	Narration	Doc No.	F Mt
30/12/2017	▾	DR TO	▾	Accountanc (157) ▾				6	12
30/12/2017	▾	CR FROM	▾	Loan4	(228) ▾			6	12

2F 2 Entry Form ⓘ

This form comes with some information but it should be edited to exactly match what is on the Loan Agreement. It comes with an **editable date** and Financial Month 12, based on the Financial Year set earlier. Tap the Date box to change to **31st** December. The **document** number is automated to 6, but it should be **edited to 5** since it also comes from the same Loan Agreement 5, just like the borrowed amount recorded above.

For boxes in the **accounts column**, the interest is an expense that is also recorded on the All Expenses account. Tap the Top box and type in the search box "**All**" then space, to speed the identification process. This displays the **All Expenses** account at the Top, Tap to select it. The account **From** is the Loan account 225. The recording format is like the interest is acquired in addition to the Loan. Tap the Lower box and type in the search box "**Loa**", to speed the identification process. This displays the Loan1 (225) account, Tap to select it.

Type the **Interest amount of 30** in the Top box, which automates the lower amount into a negative. The positive amount is the Debit while the negative amount is the Credit entry.

The narration or brief description to type could be **Loan Interest.** In case you record this Interest on your device, before Saving, the form should look as illustrated below;

←	2 Entry Form						ⓘ
Date	JN	Account	Amount	Narration	Doc No.	F N	
31/12/2017 ▾	DR TO ▾	All Expenses (25) ▾	30.00	Loan Interest	5	12	
31/12/2017 ▾	CR FROM ▾	Loan1 (225) ▾	-30.00	Loan Interest	5	12	

Then Tap in a blank space on the device to expose the bottom buttons. Tap the **Save and Close button**, or Close if not required. The **simplicity** here is that the only challenge with this task was selecting the accounts To and From. The rest are straight forward.

9.4   Trace Loan and Interest on Accounts

Look critically at the Transaction Numbers on the ledger report on your device, the **Numbers are blue**, which implies they are buttons. In case of an error with a transaction, tap its **blue transaction number**, which leads to the original recording form. Make the required correction and Tap the Update button.

From document 5 we extracted **transaction 5 the Loan,** and **6 the Interes**t as illustrated on the following Ledger report;

Annual General Ledger		To Trial Balance		
Dates	Narrations	Doc No	Trans No	Amount
5 All Income				
30-12-17	Stock Sales Paid	3	3	-33,570.90
5 All Income Balance				**-33,570.90**
25 All Expenses				
30-12-17	Stock Purchases Paid	2	2	17,165.00
31-12-17	Loan Interest	5	6	30.00
25 All Expenses Balance				**17,195.00**
205 Bank1				
1-12-17	Loan Acquired	5	5	1,200.00
30-12-17	Cash Deposit	4	4	29,200.00
205 Bank1 Balance				**30,400.00**
212 Cash				
1-12-17	Cash Capital	1	1	19,000.00
30-12-17	Stock Purchases Paid	2	2	-17,165.00
30-12-17	Stock Sales Paid	3	3	33,570.90
30-12-17	Cash Deposit	4	4	-29,200.00
212 Cash Balance				**6,205.90**
225 Loan1				
1-12-17	Loan Acquired	5	5	-1,200.00
31-12-17	Loan Interest	5	6	-30.00
225 Loan1 Balance				**-1,230.00**
271 Capital Added				
1-12-17	Cash Capital	1	1	-19,000.00
271 Capital Added Balance				**-19,000.00**

This is the **Annual General Ledger (AGL),** accessed by scrolling to the **Right**, tap "**9 Reports**", and tap the **AGL button**.

The Loan transaction 5 is received (debited) onto account 205 Bank 1, whose balance increases from 29,200 to 30,400. And comes from (credited to) account 225 Loan 1 whose negative balance rises from Zero to 1200 (1230 together with Interest). Because some mobile devices are

Small, there is No space to show a balance after every entry but only the **Cummulative balance at the bottom.**

The **Loan Interest transaction 6** value goes (debited) To the All Expenses account 25, whose balance increases from 17,165 to **17,195**. And comes From (credited to) account 225 Loan 1 whose negative balance rises from 1200 to 1230, which is the new size of the **Loan owed.**

9.5   Summary Trial Balance

This is designed to expose errors of Double Entry and Balancing in the General Ledger. However, it also summarizes the General Ledger. Below is the Cummulative Trial Balance after recording the Loan and December Interest;

TINY SHOP	
Jan-2017 to Dec-2017	
ANNUAL TRIAL BALANCE	**ATB**
To Quarterly TB	**FINAL BALANCES**
5 All Income	-33,570.90
25 All Expenses	17,195.00
205 Bank1	30,400.00
212 Cash	6,205.90
225 Loan1	-1,230.00
271 Capital Added	-19,000.00
Difference To Investigate	**0.00**

This is the **Annual Trial Balance (ATB),** accessed by scrolling to the **Right**, tap "**9 Reports**", and tap the **ATB button**.

According to the General Ledger report above, the Loan of 1,200 is part of the **30,400** balance on account 205 above, and part of the **1,230** balance on account 225. The Interest of 30 is part of the **17,195** balance on account 25, and part of the **1,230** balance on account 225.

Using a calculator we can confirm if the total Positives equate to the Total Negatives

Chapter 10.   PERSONAL CASH

10.1   Introduction

This is money taken from the business, for the owner's personal use and is commonly known as **Drawings**. This is legal although **it's Not a business expense and it doesn't reduce the Profit nor the Tax**. A business owner is known to pay themselves from profits made. If they pay themselves without Profit then they eat away the **Capital**. They decide when to pay themselves, but this doesn't affect the Tax since its Not a business Expense. Below is a Payment Voucher to illustrate the recording;

Tiny Shop
Payment Voucher   ⑥
Date: 30-Dec
For: Personal Cash from Business
2D   Amount   12,000.00
Paid by: Bank

10.2   Recording

For our Demo, this Drawing is for 12 months, although only recorded in month 12. The guide indicates it should be recorded using form 2D. Tapping **2D Cash for Owner** displays the following form;

Date			Account	Amount	Narration	Doc No.	F Mth	F
30/12/2017	▼	To	Owner Cash (286) ▼		Cash for Owner	6	12	4th
30/12/2017	▼	From	Cash (212) ▼		Cash for Owner	6	12	4th

This form comes with some information but should be edited to exactly match what is on the Payment Voucher. It comes with an **editable date** and Financial Month 12, based on the Financial Year set earlier. The **editable document** number is automated to 6, since it's the 6th document to be recorded.

For boxes in the **accounts column**, the document says money comes "**From**" the Bank account. Tap the Lower box to select **Bank1 205**. The money goes "**To**" a personal account which is **pre-selected** in the Top box. It's the account **286 Owner Cash before Tax**.

Type the amount of 12,000 in the Top box, which automates the lower amount into a negative. The positive amount is the Debit while the negative amount is the Credit entry.

And finally it's the narration or brief description, which can be left as is. In case you record the above Payment Voucher, before saving, the form should look as illustrated below;

←	Cash for Owner					ⓘ
Date	Account	Amount	Narration	Doc No.	F Mth	F Q
30/12/2017 ▾ To	Owner Cash (286) ▾	12000	Cash for Owner	6	12	4th
30/12/2017 ▾ From	Bank1 (205) ▾	-12000	Cash for Owner	6	12	4th

Then Tap in a blank space on the device to expose the bottom buttons. Tap the **Save and Close button**, or Close if not required. This recording is then displayed on all reports to which it applies to, like General Ledger, Trial Balance, and many others.

The **simplicity** here is that the only challenge with this task was selecting the **account From**. The rest are automated apart from the amount.

10.3   Trace Drawings on Accounts

All transactions are posted to Ledger accounts. The Bank account where the Cash came **From,** its recorded as a negative (credited) and its **balance is reduced by the 12,000.** While on the personal account which received the money, its recorded as a positive (debited) and **its balance increases**. Below is an illustration;

205 Bank1				
1-12-17	Loan Acquired	5	5	1,200.00
30-12-17	Cash Deposit	4	4	29,200.00
30-12-17	Cash for Owner	6	7	-12,000.00
205 Bank1 Balance				**18,400.00**
212 Cash				
1-12-17	Cash Capital	1	1	19,000.00
30-12-17	Stock Purchases Paid	2	2	-17,165.00
30-12-17	Stock Sales Paid	3	3	33,570.90
30-12-17	Cash Deposit	4	4	-29,200.00
212 Cash Balance				**6,205.90**
225 Loan1				
1-12-17	Loan Acquired	5	5	-1,200.00
31-12-17	Loan Interest	5	6	-30.00
225 Loan1 Balance				**-1,230.00**
271 Capital Added				
1-12-17	Cash Capital	1	1	-19,000.00
271 Capital Added Balance				**-19,000.00**
286 Owner Cash Before Tax				
30-12-17	Cash for Owner	6	7	12,000.00
286 Owner Cash Before Tax Balance				**12,000.00**

This is the **Annual General Ledger (AGL),** accessed by scrolling to the **Right**, tap "**9 Reports**", and tap the **AGL button**.

According to the recording of document 6 which is transaction 7, the value left the 205 Bank1 account and it's balance fell to 18,400 since it's the source of money. The value ends up on account 286 Owners Cash before Tax and it's balance rises from Zero to 12,000. Please Note there is account **287** for recording **Owner's Cash after Tax**. The difference is Not important at this stage.

In case of an error with any of the above transactions, tap the **blue transaction number**, which takes you to the original recording form. Make the required correction and Tap the Update button.

10.4   Drawings on Summary Trial Balance

Although the Trial Balance balances after every recording, **the balances for the 2 affected accounts do change**. Below is the Cummulative Trial Balance after recording Drawings;

TINY SHOP	
Jan-2017 to Dec-2017	
ANNUAL TRIAL BALANCE	**ATB**
To Quarterly TB	**FINAL BALANCES**
5 All Income	-33,570.90
25 All Expenses	17,195.00
205 Bank1	18,400.00
212 Cash	6,205.90
225 Loan1	-1,230.00
271 Capital Added	-19,000.00
286 Owner Cash Before Tax	12,000.00
Difference To Investigate	**0.00**

This is the **Annual Trial Balance (ATB),** accessed by scrolling to the **Right**, tap "**9 Reports**", and tap the **ATB button**.

According to the General Ledger accounts above, the **Debit of 12,000** is the balance on account 286. The **Credit entry** is part of the Bank1 balance which was reduced to 18,400. We can confirm by looking and calculating the balance on account 205.

Using a calculator we can confirm if the total Positives equate to the Total Negatives.

11.1   Introduction

Most businesses rent premises where they operate from, and the smaller businesses pay this by Cash. Below is a receipt used to illustrate the recording of this expense;

```
                        Landlord              (7)
  Receipt                    Date: 01-Dec
  Details:    Rent
              2B             Amount    4,800.00
  Paid by:           Cash
```

11.2   Recording

This expense was paid on the first using Cash. The guide indicates it should be recorded using form 2B. Tapping **2B All Allowable Expenses** displays the following form;

Date	Account	Amount	Narration	Doc No.	F Mth	F
30/12/2017 ▼	All Expenses (25) ▼		All Expenses	7	12	4tl
30/12/2017 ▼	Cash (212) ▼		All Expenses	7	12	4tl

All Allowable Expenses ⓘ

This form comes with some information but should be edited to exactly match what is on the expense receipt. It comes with an **editable date** and Financial Month 12, based on the Financial Year set earlier. Tap the Date box to change to **1st** December. The **editable document** number is automated to 7, since it's the **7th** document to be recorded.

The pre-selected expense in the Top box is the **desired account 25 for All Expenses.** And the Lower box has the **default paying account** which is Cash. No modification for the 2.

Type the amount of 4,800 in the Top box, which automates the lower amount into a negative. The positive amount is the Debit while the negative amount is the Credit entry.

The narration or brief description could be modified to **Rent.** In case you record this expense on your device, before Saving, the form should look as illustrated below;

Date	Account	Amount	Narration	Doc No.	F Mth	F Q
01/12/2017 ▼	All Expenses (25) ▼	4800.00	Rent	7	12	4th
01/12/2017 ▼	Cash (212) ▼	-4800.00	Rent	7	12	4th

All Allowable Expenses ⓘ

Then Tap in a blank space on the device to expose the bottom buttons. Tap the **Save and Close button**, or Close if not required. The simplicity with this task is that we only modified the Date and Narration, typed the amount, and the rest are automated.

11.3   Trace Rent on Accounts

Copied from document 7, recorded using form 2B, Rent Paid ends up on the selected account **From** and account **To** as illustrated below;

25 All Expenses				
1-12-17	Rent Paid	7	3	4,800.00
30-12-17	Stock Purchases Paid	2	2	17,165.00
31-12-17	Loan Interest	5	5	30.00
25 All Expenses Balance				**21,995.00**

205 Bank1				
1-12-17	Loan Acquired	5	5	1,200.00
30-12-17	Cash Deposit	4	4	29,200.00
30-12-17	Cash for Owner	6	7	-12,000.00
205 Bank1 Balance				**18,400.00**

212 Cash				
1-12-17	Cash Capital	1	1	19,000.00
1-12-17	Rent Paid	7	8	-4,800.00
30-12-17	Stock Purchases Paid	2	2	-17,165.00
30-12-17	Stock Sales Paid	3	3	33,570.90
30-12-17	Cash Deposit	4	4	-29,200.00
212 Cash Balance				**1,405.90**

This is the **Annual General Ledger (AGL),** accessed by scrolling to the **Right**, tap "**9 Reports**", and tap the **AGL button**.

The transaction number generated by the software is **8.** We see the **4800** recorded onto account 25 All Expenses as a positive since that is where the value went **To**, increasing the balance or Total Expenses to 21,995. And the same amount seen as a negative **From** the Cash account which paid, reducing its balance to 1,405.90

In case of an error with any of the above records, tap the **blue transaction number**, which leads to the original recording form. Make the required correction and Tap the Update button.

11.4   Summary Trial Balance

Although the above illustration shows the To and From records for Rent Paid, it doesn't show all the Ledger accounts for this Demo. However, if we copied all balances on the 7 accounts after recording Rent, we end up with the following Trial Balance;

TINY SHOP	
Jan-2017 to Dec-2017	
ANNUAL TRIAL BALANCE	**ATB**
To Quarterly TB	**FINAL BALANCES**
5 All Income	-33,570.90
25 All Expenses	21,995.00
205 Bank1	18,400.00
212 Cash	1,405.90
225 Loan1	-1,230.00
271 Capital Added	-19,000.00
286 Owner Cash Before Tax	12,000.00
Difference To Investigate	**0.00**

This is the **Annual Trial Balance (ATB),** accessed by scrolling to the **Right**, tap "**9 Reports**", and tap the **ATB button**.

According to the Ledger accounts above, the Rent paid is part of the **21,995** balance on the **25 All Expenses account**, and part of the **1405.90** balance on account **212 Cash**.

The Zero difference at the bottom confirms the Total Positives equate the Total Negatives, and this can be confirmed using a calculator.

Please Note: Form 2B is the one used to record All Payments and Purchases made for business purposes, for an individual business Not Vat registered. This includes: Reselling Stock, Raw Materials, Other Direct Costs, Insurance, Advertising, Free Samples, Website Costs, Subscriptions to Trade or Professional bodies/ Journals, Stationery, Printing, Postage, Ink & Cartridges, Rent, Business & Water Rates, Utility bills, Insurance, Security, Home Office, Repairs & Maintenance of Business Premises & Equipment
Vehicles: Insurance, Maintenance, Fuel, Parking, Hire Charges, Licence, breakdown cover, Travel Tickets & Taxi Fares, Hotel & Meals on Overnight Business Trips, Uniforms, Protective Clothing, Costumes, Employee & Staff salaries, bonuses, pensions, benefits, Agency Fees, Sub-Contractors, Employers NI, Accountancy, Solicitors, Surveyors, Architects Fees, Bank Overdraft and Credit Card charges, Interest on Loans and Hire Purchases, leasing.

This Excludes: Products For Personal Use, Non Business driving or Travel Costs, Fines for Breaking the Law, Travel between Home and Work.

12.1   Introduction

After Cash is deposited with the Bank, it has to be withdrawn whenever part of it is required for the business. It can be drawn from a Cash machine without any documentation, or from inside a Bank where a Withdraw slip is filled in. Below is a Cash Withdraw slip to illustrate the recording;

```
Natwest Bank                                    ( 8 )
               CASH WITHDRAW
        2C                      Date: 30-Dec
               Account Number          774174

    Name:      Tiny Shop
                          Amount      120.00
    Signature: _____
```

12.2   Recording

The **business name and account number** are indicated. The guide indicates it should be recorded using form 2C. Tapping **2C Bank Deposit, Withdraw & Transfer** displays the following form;

Date		Account		Amount	Narration	Doc No.	F M
30/12/2017 ▾	To	Cash	(212) ▾			8	12
30/12/2017 ▾	From	Bank1	(205) ▾			8	12

This form comes with some information but should be edited to exactly match what is on the Withdraw Slip. It comes with an **editable date** and Financial Month 12, based on the Financial Year set earlier. The **editable document** number is **automated to 8**, since it's the 8th document to be recorded.

For boxes in the **accounts column**, the money comes "**From**" Bank account, which is **pre-selected** in the Lower box. The money goes "**To**" the Cash account which is **also pre-selected** in the Top box. None is changed and **time is saved**.

Type the amount of 120 in the Top box, which automates the lower amount into a negative. The positive amount is the Debit while the negative amount is the Credit recording.

And finally it's the narration or brief description which should be; **Cash Withdraw**. In case you record the above Deposit Slip, before saving, the form should look as illustrated below;

Bank Deposit, Withdraw & Transfers					ⓘ
Date	**Account**	**Amount**	**Narration**	**Doc No.**	**F Mth**
30/12/2017 ▾ To	Cash (212) ▾	120.00	Cash Withdraw|	8	12
30/12/2017 ▾ From	Bank1 (205) ▾	-120.00	Cash Withdraw	8	12

Then Tap in a blank space on the device to expose the bottom buttons. Tap the **Save and Close button**, or Close if not required. The simplicity here is that we only typed the amount and Narration.

12.3 Trace Cash Withdraw on Accounts
Copied from document 8, recorded using form 2C, Cash Withdraw ends up on the selected account **From** and account **To** as illustrated below;

The Bank account where the Cash came is **credited** and its **balance is reduced by the 120**. While the Cash account which **received the money is debited and its balance increases**. Below is an illustration;

205 Bank1				
1-12-17	Loan Acquired	5	5	1,200.00
30-12-17	Cash Deposit	4	4	29,200.00
30-12-17	Cash for Owner	6	7	-12,000.00
30-12-17	Cash Withdraw	8	9	-120.00
205 Bank1 Balance				**18,280.00**

212 Cash				
1-12-17	Cash Capital	1	1	19,000.00
1-12-17	Rent Paid	7	3	-4,800.00
30-12-17	Stock Purchases Paid	2	2	-17,165.00
30-12-17	Stock Sales Paid	3	3	33,570.90
30-12-17	Cash Deposit	4	4	-29,200.00
30-12-17	Cash Withdraw	8	9	120.00
212 Cash Balance				**1,525.90**

The transaction number generated by the software is **number 9.** We see the **120** recorded onto account **212 Cash** as a positive since that is where the value went **To**, increasing the balance to **1,525.90**. And the same amount seen as a negative **From** the **205 Bank1** account, reducing its balance to 18,280

In case of an error with any of the above records, tap the **blue transaction number**, which leads to the original recording form. Make the required correction and Tap the Update button.

12.4   Summary Trial Balance

Although the above illustration shows the To and From records for Cash Withdraw, it doesn't show all the Ledger accounts for this Demo. However, if we copied all balances on the 7 accounts after recording the Cash Withdraw, we end up with the following Trial Balance;

TINY SHOP				
Jan-2017 to Dec-2017				
C1		THE FINAL TRIAL BALANCE		
Year End Adjustments added to Year End Balances to get the Final Balances				
To Journals To Quarterly	YE BALANCES	YE ADJUSTMENTS	FINAL BALANCES	
5 All Income	-33,570.90	0.00	-33,570.90	
25 All Expenses	21,995.00	0.00	21,995.00	
205 Bank1	18,280.00	0.00	18,280.00	
212 Cash	1,525.90	0.00	1,525.90	
225 Loan1	-1,230.00	0.00	-1,230.00	
271 Capital Added	-19,000.00	0.00	-19,000.00	
286 Owner Cash Before Tax	12,000.00	0.00	12,000.00	
Difference To Investigate	**0.00**	**0.00**	**0.00**	

According to the Ledger accounts above, the 120 Cash Withdraw is **part of the Cash balance** which was increased to 1,525.90. It's also **part of the Bank1 balance** which was reduced to **18,280**.

The **Zero difference** at the bottom confirms the Total Positives equate the Total Negatives, and this can be confirmed using a calculator

13.1 Introduction

This business bought an Android Tablet for recording its business transactions and print reports. This should be a **Fixed Asset** since it's to last atleast 2 years. However, since it's a **small business Not Registered for Vat**, the UK allows it to write off Fixed Assets in the year of purchase, and recorded as Expenses. This includes Computers, Other Equipment, and Vehicles used for only 2 years (But Not Cars). So this Tablet is effectively recorded as an expense. Below is a receipt used to illustrate the recording of this Asset/ Expense;

	PC Store	9
Receipt		Date: 01-Dec
Details:	Android Tablet	
	Net Amount	450.00
2B	Vat	90.00
	Total	540.00
Paid by:	Bank	

13.2 Recording

This Tablet was bought on the first using a Debit Card for the Bank account. The guide indicates it should be recorded using form 2B. Tapping **2B All Allowable Expenses** displays the following form;

All Allowable Expenses					
Date	Account	Amount	Narration	Doc No.	F M
30/12/2017 ▼	All Expenses (25) ▼		All Expenses	9	12
30/12/2017 ▼	Cash (212) ▼		All Expenses	9	12

This form comes with some information but should be edited to exactly match what's on the purchase receipt. It comes with an **editable date** and Financial Month 12, based on the Financial Year set earlier. Tap the Date box to change to **1st** December. The **editable document** number is automated to 9, since it's the **9th** document to be recorded.

The **pre-selected expense** in the Top box is the desired account 25 for All Expenses. Tap the Lower box to **select Bank1 which paid**.

The business doesn't separate or claim Vat since **it's Not Vat Registered.** So type the **Vat inclusive amount of 540** in the Top box, which automates the lower amount into a negative. The positive amount is the Debit while the negative amount is the Credit entry.

The narration or brief description could be modified to **Android Tablet.** In case you record this expense on your device, before Saving, the form should look as illustrated below;

Date		Account		Amount	Narration	Doc No.	F Mth	F Quar
01/12/2017	▼	All Expenses (25)	▼	540.00	Android Tablet	9	12	4th QT
01/12/2017	▼	Bank1 (205)	▼	-540.00	Android Tablet	9	12	4th QT

Then Tap in a blank space on the device to expose the bottom buttons. Tap the **Save and Close button**, or Close if not required. The simplicity of this task is that we modify the Date, select the paying account, type the amount, and modify the narration.

13.3   Trace Tablet on Accounts
Copied from document 9, recorded using form 2B, the Tablet expense ends up on the selected account **From** and account **To** as illustrated below;

25 All Expenses				
1-12-17	Rent Paid	7	8	4,800.00
1-12-17	Android Tablet	9	10	540.00
30-12-17	Stock Purchases Paid	2	2	17,165.00
31-12-17	Loan Interest	5	6	30.00
25 All Expenses Balance				**22,535.00**
205 Bank1				
1-12-17	Loan Acquired	5	5	1,200.00
1-12-17	Android Tablet	9	10	-540.00
30-12-17	Cash Deposit	4	4	29,200.00
30-12-17	Cash for Owner	6	7	-12,000.00
30-12-17	Cash Withdraw	8	9	-120.00
205 Bank1 Balance				**17,740.00**

This is the **Annual General Ledger (AGL),** accessed by scrolling to the **Right**, tap "**9 Reports**", and tap the **AGL button.**

The transaction number generated is **10**. We see the **540** recorded onto account 25 All Expenses as a positive since that is where the value went **To**, increasing the balance or Total Expenses to **22,535**. And the same amount seen as a negative **From** the **205 Bank1** account which paid, reducing its balance to **17,740**.

In case of an error with any of the above transact ons, tap the **blue transaction number**, which leads to the original recording form. Make the required correction and Tap the Update button.

13.4   Cummulative Trial Balance
Although the above illustration shows the To and From records for Rent Paid, it doesn't show all the Ledger accounts for this Demo. However, if we copied all balances on the 7 accounts after recording the Tablet Expense, we end up with the following Trial Balance;

TINY SHOP	
Jan-2017 to Dec-2017	
ANNUAL TRIAL BALANCE	**ATB**
To Quarterly TB	**FINAL BALANCES**
5 All Income	-33,570.90
25 All Expenses	22,535.00
205 Bank1	17,740.00
212 Cash	1,525.90
225 Loan1	-1,230.00
271 Capital Added	-19,000.00
286 Owner Cash Before Tax	12,000.00
Difference To Investigate	**0.00**

This is the **Annual Trial Balance (ATB),** accessed by scrolling to the **Right**, tap "**9 Reports**", and tap the **ATB button**.

According to the Ledger accounts above, the paid Tablet is displayed as part of the **22,535** balance on account **25 All Expenses**. It's also part of the **17,740** balance on **account 205**.

The Zero difference at the bottom confirms the Total Positives equate the Total Negatives, and this can be confirmed using a calculator.

14.1   Introduction

Business Tax in the UK is based on the amount of Profit showed on the Profit and Loss account. So if there is No Profit then No Tax is Payable. If Tax was paid in previous years then there is a possibility of a Refund if a Loss is made. Some countries simply assess or determine the Tax arbitrarily. Whatever method is used, although **Tax is Not a business expense and doesn't appear on the Profit and Loss account**, it has an **impact on the Cash balance and the Owner's Equity**. Below is a Payment Voucher to illustrate the recording of Tax Paid.

Tiny Shop	10
Payment Voucher	
Date:	31-Dec
For: **Final Tax Paid**	
2F **Amount**	1,500.00
Paid by: Cash	

14.2   Recording

The guide on this Voucher is to use form 2F. Tap the **2F 2 Entry Form** button to expose the following;

Date		JN	Account	Amount	Narration	Doc No.	F Mth	F Qu
30/12/2017	DR TO		Accountanc (157) ▼			10	12	4th Q
30/12/2017	CR FROM		Loan4 (228) ▼			10	12	4th Q

This form comes with some information but should be edited to exactly match what is on the Payment Voucher. It comes with an **editable date** and Financial Month 12, based on the Financial Year set earlier. Tap the Date box to change to **31st** December, which is the last Date of the Financial Year. The **editable document** number is automated to 10, since it's the **10th** document to be recorded.

For boxes in the **accounts column**, the effect is value coming "**From**" the Cash account which Paid, "**To**" the Tax Paid account which received the value. So Tap the Top box and type "**Tax**" in the search box to speed up the identification process. This displays various account names with the word **Tax**. The most appropriate to select is "**Final Tax Paid (281)**" since it's paid and it's the final Tax for the year, it's Not a part Payment. Then Tap the Lower dropdown, type "**Cash**" in the search box to speed the selection of Cash 212, which is the account where the payment came **From**.

Type the Tax amount of **1,500** in the Top box, which automates the lower amount into a negative. The positive amount is the Debit while the negative amount is the Credit entry. The narration or brief description to type could be **"Tax Paid"**.

In case you record this Tax on your device, before saving, the form should look as illustrated below;

←		2 Entry Form						ⓘ
Date	JN	Account	Amount	Narration	Doc No.	F Mth	
31/12/2017 ▾ DR TO ▾		Final Tax Pa (281) ▾	1500.00	Tax Paid	10	12	4
31/12/2017 ▾ CR FROM ▾		Cash (212) ▾	-1500.00	Tax Paid	10	12	4

Then Tap in a blank space on the device to expose the bottom buttons. Tap the **Save and Close button**, or Close if not required. This transaction or its value then appears on all reports it applies to, like General Ledger, Trial Balance, and many others.

14.3   Trace on Accounts

Copied from Payment Voucher 10, recorded using form 2F, the Tax Paid ends up on the selected account **From** and account **To** as illustrated below;

212 Cash				
1-12-17	Cash Capital	1	1	19,000.00
1-12-17	Rent Paid	7	8	-4,800.00
30-12-17	Stock Purchases Paid	2	2	-17,165.00
30-12-17	Stock Sales Paid	3	3	33,570.90
30-12-17	Cash Deposit	4	4	-29,200.00
30-12-17	Cash Withdraw	8	9	120.00
31-12-17	Tax Paid	10	11	-1,500.00
212 Cash Balance				**25.90**

281 Final Tax Paid				
31-12-17	Tax Paid	10	11	1,500.00
281 Final Tax Paid Balance				**1,500.00**

The auto transaction number generated by the software is **11**. We see the **1,500** recorded onto account **281 Final Tax Paid** as a positive since that is where the value went **To**, increasing the balance to **1,500**. And the same amount seen as a negative **From** the **212 Cash** account which paid, reducing its balance to **25.90**.

In case of an error with any of the above transactions, tap the **blue transaction number**, which takes you to the original recording form. Make the required correction and Tap the Update button.

14.4   Cummulative Trial Balance

Although the above illustration shows the To and From records for Rent Paid, it doesn't show all the Ledger accounts for this Demo. However, if we copied all balances on the 8 accounts after recording the Final Tax Paid, we end up with the following Trial Balance;

TINY SHOP	
Jan-2017 to Dec-2017	
ANNUAL TRIAL BALANCE	**ATB**
To Quarterly TB	**FINAL BALANCES**
5 All Income	-33,570.90
25 All Expenses	22,535.00
205 Bank1	17,740.00
212 Cash	25.90
225 Loan1	-1,230.00
271 Capital Added	-19,000.00
281 Final Tax Paid	1,500.00
286 Owner Cash Before Tax	12,000.00
Difference To Investigate	**0.00**

According to the Ledger accounts above, the paid Tax of 1500 is displayed as part of the **1,500** balance on account **281 Tax Paid**. It's also part of the **25.90** balance on **account 212 Cash**.

The Zero difference at the bottom confirms the Total Positives equate the Total Negatives, and this can be confirmed using a calculator.

Chapter 15.   CASH REGISTER

Cash Register is a monthly report which shows d**etails of Cash Received and Paid Out** by the main Cash account number **212**. It also shows the **Opening Balance** at the start of the Month, plus **daily balances** at the end of each day.

It's aimed at providing a facility for the **instant monitoring of the Cash balance**, and providing an expected figure at the end of each Day. Basing on the accuracy of recorded information, the expected balance can be confirmed against the physical Cash available at any time of the Day. And this helps to immediately **expose lost Cash**, not to go unnoticed. Below is an illustration for Tiny Shop;

TINY SHOP

Jan-2017 to Dec-2017

Dates	Narrations	Doc No	Trans No	CS Amount
	Cash Register (Account 212) - Month 12			CS
	Balance Bf			0.00
1-12-17				
1-12-17	Rent	7	8	-4,800.00
1-12-17 Balance				**-4,800.00**
30-12-17				
30-12-17	Money Capital	1	1	19,000.00
30-12-17	Stock Purchases Paid	2	2	-17,165.00
30-12-17	Stock Sales Paid	3	3	33,570.90
30-12-17	Cash Deposit	4	4	-29,200.00
30-12-17	Cash Withdraw	8	9	120.00
30-12-17 Balance				**1,525.90**
31-12-17				
31-12-17	Tax Paid	10	11	-1,500.00
31-12-17 Balance				**25.90**

This Register starts with an awkward position of paying before any Cash is received. However, that should be ignored since the month end position makes sense. Cash Paid out is indicted with a minus sign, while Cash received is a positive without any sign. We can confirm the balance using a calculator, by adding the Received positive figures and deducting the Paid negative amounts.

Although very similar, the function of this report may not be played by the **Cash account** in the Ledger Book since it doesn't show balances at the end of each Day. However, the balance on this report should be the same as the one on any Cash report or balance generated by the software.

This report is located in section **2 MISC**, just below the Dashboard. On tapping the button, the Cash Register for month 1 is displayed. Tap the dropdown to select month 12 to view the above report.

Chapter 16 <u>FINAL REPORTS AND SUPPORT</u>

Page

16.1　Introduction

Our Demo business has only 10 documents, although they are supposed to be representative for a whole Year. None of the 23 Period Reports are looked at, we instead look at the **General Ledger** for the whole year. Out of **13 Stock Reports** we look at the **ST1** Stock Information, **ST5** Stock Movement, **ST11** Annual Sales and Profit, plus **ST13** Stock Taking List. Out of **80 Annual Reports**, only the **ATB** Annual Trial Balance, **B4** Notes to Financial Statements, **B1** Profit and Loss account, **B2** Balance Sheet, and **A1** Short Tax Return are looked at. Plus the **Dashboard**.

If businesses were allowed to **pluck figures from thin air**, All Income would be eaten away by Expenses and nobody would pay **Tax**. But Governments need Tax Revenue. So the **Law** requires that **All records in Accounting must be based or supported by source documents.** And although business Records submitted to Tax Authorities are in Summary form, businesses **MUST keep detailed records for some years**, in case Tax Authorities need to confirm some information. Therefore, as we wind up this module training, we look at how a Tax Report is supported by Reports and Documents. Below is an illustration of the chain of support;

From Documents To Tax Report

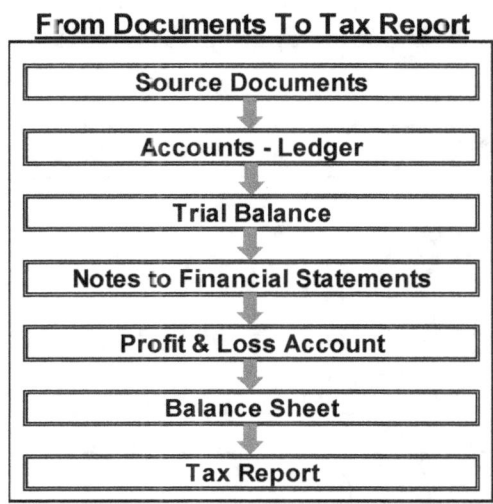

It's because of the need to **support the Tax Report or Summary Accounting Records** that **many reports** are provided, making it **self-explanatory** to those who require and understand them.

16.2   Accounts From Documents

Transactions are copied from source documents and recorded onto Accounts in the Ledger. Therefore, it's the **filed source documents which support the records on Accounts.** Below is an illustration of Accounts Records supported by source documents;

TINY SHOP

Jan-2017 to Dec-2017

Dates	Narrations	Doc No	Trans No	Amount
	Annual General Ledger		To Trial Balance	
5 All Income				
30-12-17	Stock Sales Paid	3	3	-33,570.90
5 All Income Balance				-33,570.90
25 All Expenses				
1-12-17	Rent Paid	7	8	4,800.00
1-12-17	Android Tablet	9	10	540.00
30-12-17	Stock Purchases Paid	2	2	17,165.00
31-12-17	Loan Interest	5	6	30.00
25 All Expenses Balance				22,535.00
205 Bank1				
1-12-17	Loan Acquired	5	5	1,200.00
1-12-17	Android Tablet	9	10	-540.00
30-12-17	Cash Deposit	4	4	29,200.00
30-12-17	Cash for Owner	6	7	-12,000.00
30-12-17	Cash Withdraw	8	9	-120.00
205 Bank1 Balance				17,740.00
212 Cash				
1-12-17	Cash Capital	1	1	19,000.00
1-12-17	Rent Paid	7	8	-4,800.00
30-12-17	Stock Purchases Paid	2	2	-17,165.00
30-12-17	Stock Sales Paid	3	3	33,570.90
30-12-17	Cash Deposit	4	4	-29,200.00
30-12-17	Cash Withdraw	8	9	120.00
31-12-17	Tax Paid	10	11	-1,500.00
212 Cash Balance				25.90

225 Loan1				
1-12-17	Loan Acquired	5	5	-1,200.00
31-12-17	Loan Interest	5	6	-30.00
225 Loan1 Balance				**-1,230.00**
271 Capital Added				
1-12-17	Cash Capital	1	1	-19,000.00
271 Capital Added Balance				**-19,000.00**
281 Final Tax Paid				
31-12-17	Tax Paid	10	11	1,500.00
281 Final Tax Paid Balance				**1,500.00**
286 Owner Cash Before Tax				
30-12-17	Cash for Owne᷍	6	7	12,000.00
286 Owner Cash Before Tax Balance				**12,000.00**

The above Accounts are found ir section **9 Reports, Ta͗p Annual General Ledger.** For each record on an acɔount, we must indicate the number of the document where it's extracted from. In case of any queries, that document is sought, following a good filing systɛm, as explained in Module 2. Following the indicated **document number** (not Transaction number) for each record above, lets confirm if they are each supporƚed by one of the 10 documents below;

Tiny Shop ①
Receipt Date: 01-Dec
  For: Owner's Investment
    2E Amount 19,000.00
Rcvd by: Cash

Natwest Bank ④
Deposit Slip No: 56
Date: 30-Dec
  2C Cash Total 29,200.00

FUN Mobiles ②
RECEIPT To: Tiny Shop

Items	Price	QTY	Net Cost
	Stock	Date:	30-᷍ec
Sony	125.00	25	3,125.00
Nokia	309.00	25	7,725.00
Iphone	147.00	25	3,675.00
Galaxy	88.00	30	2,640.00
3C	Total Amount		17,165.00
Paid by:	Cash		

TINY SᴴOP ③
Cash Sales RECEIꟼT

Items	Price	QTY	Net Cost
		Date:	30-Dec
Sony	321.20	18	5,781.60
Nokia	543.40	24	13,041.60
Iphone	386.10	17	6,563.70
Galaxy	272.80	30	8,184.00
3A	Total Amount		33,570.90
Paid by:	Cash		

LCAN AGREEMENT ⑤ LN: 743
Borrower: **Tiny Shop** Date: 01-Dec
  ᷍ɔ Bank Account
Amount: **1,200.00** 7A Period: **12 Months**
  31-Dec
Monthly Interest: **30.00** ᷍F Monthly Total Repayment: **130.00**
Total Interest: **360.00** Repayments Start: **31-Dec**

```
┌─────────────────────────────────────┐     ┌─────────────────────────────────────┐
│            Tiny Shop                 │     │            Landlord          ⑦      │
│  Payment Voucher          ⑥         │     │  Receipt          Date: 01-Dec     │
│              Date: 30-Dec            │     │  Details:    Rent                   │
│  For: Personal Cash from Business    │     │      2B           Amount  4,800.00 │
│  2D         Amount  12,000.00        │     │  Paid by:         Cash              │
│  Paid by:              Bank          │     └─────────────────────────────────────┘
└─────────────────────────────────────┘
```

```
┌─────────────────────────────────────┐     ┌─────────────────────────────────────┐
│  Natwest Bank             ⑧         │     │            PC Store          ⑨      │
│       CASH WITHDRAW Slip             │     │  Receipt          Date: 01-Dec     │
│    2C          Date: 30-Dec          │     │  Details:   Android Tablet          │
│         Account Number     774174    │     │               Net Amount    450.00 │
│  Name:    Tiny Shop                  │     │      2B            Vat        90.00 │
│              Amount    120.00        │     │               Total         540.00 │
│  Signature:                          │     │  Paid by:         Bank              │
└─────────────────────────────────────┘     └─────────────────────────────────────┘
```

```
            ┌─────────────────────────────────────┐
            │            Tiny Shop        ⑩       │
            │  Payment Voucher                     │
            │        Date:            31-Dec       │
            │     For:      Final Tax Paid         │
            │       2F         Amount   1,500.00   │
            │  Paid by:        Cash                │
            └─────────────────────────────────────┘
```

Please contact us if any of them is not supported.

16.3   Trial Balance From Accounts in Ledger

It's the **balances** on each and every account in the Ledger, which are listed to come up with the **Trial Balance**. So the Ledger is **summarized** to come up with the Trial Balance. Therefore, **each of the balances on the Trial Balance is supported by a Ledger account.** Below is the Final Annual Trial Balance for TINY SHOP;

TINY SHOP	
Jan-2017 to Dec-2017	
ANNUAL TRIAL BALANCE	**ATB**
To Quarterly TB	**FINAL BALANCES**
5 All Income	-33,570.90
25 All Expenses	22,535.00
205 Bank1	17,740.00
212 Cash	25.90
225 Loan1	-1,230.00
271 Capital Added	-19,000.00
281 Final Tax Paid	1,500.00
286 Owner Cash Before Tax	12,000.00
Difference To Investigate	0.00

This is found in section **9 Reports,** and tap the **ATB button**.

This Demo doesn't have Adjustments, so ignore the middle column. We should confirm if each of these balances is supported by a Ledger account above. If that's true, then we have provided an explanation for each of the balances, and it's therefore, supported.

However, although the ATB is a Summary of the General Ledger, it also **confirms the absence of Double Entry and balancing errors**. As to why we refer to it as a Final Trial Balance, we also have Period and Cummulative Trial Balances.

16.4   Notes from Annual Trial Balance

Notes to Financial Statements are lists of balances prepared to show how the Total figures presented on Financial Statements are arrived at. This is done because of the need to **summarize** the **180** Income and Expense account balances into **16 figures for the Profit and Loss account**. And to summarize the **120** Assets, Liabilities and Equity accounts into **14 figures for the Balance Sheet**. Therefore, for all the **300** Ledger accounts, we summarise them into **30 Notes or groups of balances**. However, groups without any balances are Not displayed, and accounts without balances are also Not listed. Each of the Notes indicates the accounts range of balances it's supposed to **display and add**.

On the following Page is Report B4 Notes to Financial Statements for TINY SHOP, basing on the few recorded documents and accounts.

The account balances below are grouped basing on the layout of the **Tax Report** designed by the Tax Authority, which determines our **layout** of the **Profit and Loss account and Balance Sheet,** where the figures are **copied** from. Basing on the layout of the summary Profit and Loss account, we decide which Income account is listed first and which one last, in the Ledger. This also determines which Expense account comes first and which one last, plus which accounts should be **next to each other**, since they are summed up to get a total for the Profit and Loss account. For example, the **Main Income accounts** are allocated accounts **1 to 10**, and their balances are added up in **Note 1**, to get the **Turnover figure** for the Profit and Loss account. There is more of this in training **Modules 2, 3 and 4**.

However, since the recorded documents for this Demo generate only a few scattered balances according to their account numbering, No grouping is displayed by the following **B4 Notes to Financial**

Statements;

TINY SHOP			
Jan-2017 to Dec-2017			**B4**
Notes To Financial Statements on B1 & B2			
		Most Recent Year	**Previous Year**
Note 01: Turnover (1-10)			
5 All Income	F2	-33,570.90	0.00
Note 1 Total		-33,570.90	0.00
Note 03: Cost of Sales (21-44)			
25 All Expenses	G3	22,535.00	0.00
Note 3 Total		22,535.00	0.00
Note 21: Bank Balances (205-11)			
205 Bank1	L2	17,740.00	0.00
Note 21 Total		17,740.00	0.00
Note 22: Cash Balance (212-3)			
212 Cash	M1	25.90	0.00
Note 22 Total		25.90	0.00
Note 25: Loans & Hire Purchases (225-30)			
225 Loan1	R4	-1,230.00	0.00
Note 25 Total		-1,230.00	0.00
Note 28: Capital Added (271-79)			
271 Capital Added	T2	-19,000.00	0.00
Note 28 Total		-19,000.00	0.00
Note 29: Tax on Profit (280-85)			
281 Final Tax Paid	T3	1,500.00	0.00
Note 29 Total		1,500.00	0.00
Note 30: Drawings (286-98)			
286 Owner Cash Before Tax	T4	12,000.00	0.00
Note 30 Total		12,000.00	0.00

This B4 Report is found in section **9 Reports, Year End Reports,** Tap **B Financial Statements & Notes,** and finally **B4 Notes to Financial Statements**.

Each of the above Notes indicates the account ranges which are normally added, although none of them has more than 1 balance, since it's a small Demo. However, this is illustrated better in Modules 2, 3, and 4.

Please Note the **ATB is a Summary report** which doesn't provide any detail as far as any of the above balances is concerned. However, it's the most reliable source of figures which **confirms that each value was recorded twice, and that the balancing of accounts has No errors.**

Since the ATB is a Summary, we instead **use the detailed Ledger accounts to support the balances on B4 Notes**. Accounts 212 and 205 have several transactions but the best illustration is **account 25 for All Expenses**. Where does the total of **22,535** come from? Please check account **25** on previous pages to confirm if there is **sufficient support for the Total**. Use a calculator to confirm if the figures add up. If you are satisfied then anybody else will be. And in case of need, follow up to the individual source documents indicated by their numbers. Although it's a single expense account, the **narrations specify what the money was spent on.**

16.5   Profit and Loss Account From Notes

Profit and Loss Account is a **summary statement prepared to show if the business made a profit or a loss, by deducting expenses from incomes.** It's extremely important to know if a business achieved its **primary objective of making profit.** Since it's a summary Report, the **180 balances** for incomes and expenses are reduced to just **16 figures**. Below is an illustration of the Profit and Loss Account generated for TINY SHOP;

TINY SHOP			
Jan-2017 to Dec-2017			
THE PROFIT AND LOSS ACCOUNTS			
To Balance Sheets	Notes		Most Recent Year
Gross Profit (Loss) Margin			32.87%
Net Profit (Loss) Margin			32.87%
Turnover	1		-33,570.90
Cost of Sales	3	22,535.00	
Construction Industry	4	0.00	
Cost of Sales/ Direct Expenses			22,535.00
Gross Profit (Loss)			-11,035.90
Other Income	2		0.00
Gross Income (Loss)			-11,035.90
Indirect Expenses			
Wages, Salaries and Staff Costs	5	0.00	
Motor & Travel Expenses	6	0.00	
Premises Costs	7	0.00	
Maintenance Costs	8	0.00	
Administrative Expenses	9	0.00	
Promotion and Entertainment	10	0.00	
Interest Charges	11	0.00	
Finance Charges	12	0.00	
Bad Debts	13	0.00	
Professional Costs	14	0.00	
Depreciation and Disposal	15	0.00	
Other Expenses	16	0.00	
Indirect Expenses			0.00
Net (Profit)/Loss			-11,035.90

This is found in section **9 Reports, Year End Reports,** Tap **B Financial Statements & Notes,** and finally **B1 Profit and Loss Account.**

Can we confirm that the Turnover and Cost of Sales figures come from Note 1 and Note 3 on the B4 Notes to Financial Statements, on previous pages, please verify. If that is true, then the B1 Profit and Loss account is supported by the B4 Notes to Financial Statements.

Following the **3 Line Profit and Loss accepted in the UK**, we ensured that all expenses are recorded on account 25. And that explains why we have Zeros for Notes 4 to 16. Eliminating all the above Zeros leaves a **3 Line Profit and Loss account** generated, as illustrated below;

TINY SHOP	
Jan-2017 to Dec-2017	
Dashboard Overview (YTD)	
<u>Mini Profit and Loss</u>	
Income	33,570.90
Allowable Expenses	22,535.00
Net (Profit) / Loss	**11,035.90**

This is the Top part of the **Dashboard Overview** generated by the software, found at the Top of section **2 MISC**. This is a **combined Financial Statement which shows both a mini Profit and Loss Account and mini Balance Sheet,** for the Year To Date. It gives a quick snapshot of the whole business at a glance.

The figures are the same as those on the comprehensive Profit and Loss account above, with the rest as zeros. The simple interpretation is; **All Income minus All Expenses gives the Net Profit**.

So whether it's the mini or full Profit and Loss Account, they are **supported by the same B4 Notes to Financial Statements.**

16.6   Balance Sheet From Notes

Balance Sheet is a summary statement which shows the financial position of a business by **comparing what the business owns** in form of Assets, against what it **owes in form of Liabilities and Capital or Equity**, as at a particular Date. Since it's a summary Report, the **120 balances** for Asset, Liabilities, and Equity are reduced to just **14 figures**. Below is an illustration of the Balance Sheet generated for TINY SHOP;

TINY SHOP

Jan-2017 to Dec-2017

THE BALANCE SHEETS		Most Recent Year		Previous Year
Return on Capital Employed		62.12%		%
Current Ratio		-∞:1		:1
Quick Assets Ratio		-∞:1		:1
Fixed Assets	Notes			
Equipment, Machinery & Vehicles	17		0.00	0.00
Other Fixed Assets	18		0.00	0.00
Total Fixed Assets			**0.00**	**0.00**
Current Assets				
Stock, RM & Work in Progress	19	0.00		0.00
Trade Debtors	20	0.00		0.00
Bank Balances	21	17,740.00		0.00
Cash Balances	22	25.90		0.00
Other Current Assets	23	0.00		0.00
Total Current Assets		**17,765.90**		0.00
Current Liabilities				
Trade Creditors	24	0.00		0.00
Other Current Liabs & Accurals	26	0.00		0.00
Total Current Liabilities		**0.00**		**0.00**
Net Current Assets (Liabs)			17,765.90	0.00
Total Assets less CL (CE)			**17,765.90**	**0.00**
Longterm Liabilities				
Loans & Hire Purchases	25	-1,230.00	-1,230.00	0.00
Total Liabilities		-1,230.00		0.00
NET BUSINESS ASSETS (LIABS)			16,535.90	0.00
Owner's Equity				
Capital BF	27		0.00	0.00
Capital Added	28	-19,000.00		0.00
Net Profit or Loss	PL	-11,035.90		0.00
Tax on Profit	29	1,500.00		0.00
Drawings	30	12,000.00		0.00
Net Equity Change			-16,535.90	0.00
CLOSING CAPITAL			-16,535.90	0.00
Difference to Investigate			0.00	0.00

This is found in section **9 Reports, Year End Reports,** Tap **B Financial Statements & Notes,** and finally **B2 Balance Sheet.**

Can we confirm that **Net Profit of 11,035,90** agrees with, and is supported by the **B1 Profit and Loss account**. And that the rest of the figures come from, and are supported by the **B4 Notes to Financial Statements**, as indicated by the Note numbers in their column.

At this introductory level, we can ignore the B2 Balance Sheet and focus on the Mini Balance Sheet illustrated below;

Mini Balance Sheet	
Fixed Assets	0.00
Stock and Work in Progress	0.00
Trade Debtors	0.00
Bank Balances	17,740.00
Cash Balances	25.90
Other current Assets	0.00
Total Current Assets	17,765.90
Current Liabilities	0.00
Net Current Assets (Liabilities)	17,765.90
Total Assets less CL (CE)	17,765.90
Longterm Liabilities	1,230.00
Net Business Assets (Liabilities)	16,535.90
Capital BF	0.00
Capital Added	19,000 00
Net Profit or Loss	11,035.90
Tax on Profit	1,500.00
Drawings	12,000.00
Closing Capital	16,535.90
Difference	0.00

This is the Lower part of the **Dashboard Overview** generated by the software. The figures are the same as the comprehensive Balance Sheet above.

With Zero Fixed Assets, all the Current Assets add upto to 17,765.90. Since the Liabilities are Zero, the value of Current Assets is the same as **Net Current Assets**, which is the same as **Capital Employed**. Deducting the Loan or **Long Term Liabilities** of **1,230** leaves the **Net Business Assets at 16,535.90.**

No Capital was brought forward. The Capital Invested of **19,000**, add the **Net Profit of 11,035.90,** less the **1,500 Tax on Profit**, less the **12,000 Drawings,** leaves a **Closing Capital of 16,535.90**. And this **equates** to the Net Business Assets figure above, concluding there is a **Zero difference**, and that the **Balance Sheet balances.**

It's mentioned earlier on that **Tax is Not a business expense**, which is the reason why it doesn't appear on the Profit and Loss account. It appears on the Balance Sheet as a figure that **reduces what belongs to the owner in form of Equity.** Or a **figure that reduces the amount of Profit** the owner can take from the business. So it effectively **reduces the Owner's Equity.**

16.7   Owner's Income

The middle section of the Dashboard computes the **Tax and Income** for the owner. Please remember that this version of the App is for a **Sole Trader,** whose personal Income to take Home, can be **all the Profit left after paying Tax**. So what they pay themselves is Not a business expense but **a share of the Profit Made.** As the Dashboard computes Tax, it also calculates the **Annual, monthly and weekly Income** drawable from the business. Below is an illustration;

TINY SHOP	
Jan-2017 to Dec-2017	
Dashboard Overview (YTD)	
Profit and Loss	
Income	33,570.90
Allowable Expenses	22,535.00
Net (Profit) / Loss	11,035.90
Tax & Income Update	**To Computations**
Profit to Tax (After Adjustments) ⓘ	11,035.90
Class 2 NIC	0.00
Class 4 NIC Total	0.00
Tax on Profit 20% (Est)	2,207.18
Tax on Profit 40% (Est)	0.00
Tax & NIC Outstanding (EST)	2,207.18
Year Income after Tax (EST)	8,828.72
Monthly Income (EST)	735.73
Weekly Income (EST)	169.78

If your device is computing **NIC**, stop it by ticking the box by number 37 on the computations Page. Tap the blue **Computations** button to access it. More on this in **modules 2 and 4**

Chapter 17   TAX REPORT

Below is the UK Short Tax Report submitted by the Self Employed or Sole Traders **not registered for Vat**. It's just 2 pages:

HM Revenue & Customs

Self-employment (short)

Tax year 6 April 2016 to 5 April 2017 (2016–17)

Please read the 'Self-employment (short) notes' to check if you should use this page or the 'Self-employment (full)' page.

To get notes and helpsheets that will help you fill in this form, go to www.gov.uk/self-assessment-forms-and-helpsheets

Your name

Your Unique Taxpayer Reference (UTR)

Business details

1 Description of business

2 Postcode of your business address

3 If your business name, description, address or postcode have changed in the last 12 months, put 'X' in the box and give details in the 'Any other information' box of your tax return

4 If you are a foster carer or shared lives carer, put 'X' in the box – read the notes

5 If your business started after 5 April 2016, enter the start date DD MM YYYY

6 If your business ceased before 6 April 2017, enter the final date of trading DD MM YYYY

7 Date your books or accounts are made up to – read the notes

8 If you used the cash basis, money actually received and paid out to calculate your income and expenses put 'X' in the box – read the notes

Business income – if your annual business turnover was below £83,000

9 Your turnover – the takings, fees, sales or money earned by your business

10 Any other business income not included in box 9

Allowable business expenses

If your annual turnover was below £83,000 you may just put your total expenses in box 20, rather than filling in the whole section.

11 Costs of goods bought for resale or goods used

12 Car, van and travel expenses – after private use proportion

13 Wages, salaries and other staff costs

14 Rent, rates, power and insurance costs

15 Repairs and maintenance of property and equipment

16 Accountancy, legal and other professional fees

17 Interest and bank and credit card etc financial charges

18 Phone, fax, stationery and other office costs

19 Other allowable business expenses – client entertaining costs are not an allowable expense

20 Total allowable expenses – total of boxes 11 to 19

Net profit or loss

21	Net profit - if your business income is more than your expenses (if box 9 + box 10 minus box 20 is positive)	22	Or, net loss - if your expenses exceed your business income (if box 20 minus (box 9 + box 10) is positive)
	£ . 0 0		£ . 0 0

Tax allowances for vehicles and equipment (capital allowances)

There are 'capital' tax allowances available for vehicles and equipment used in your business. (Please don't include the cost of these in your business expenses.)

23	Annual Investment Allowance	25	Other capital allowances
	£ . 0 0		£ . 0 0
24	Allowance for small balance of unrelieved expenditure	26	Total balancing charges - where you have disposed of items for more than their tax value
	£ . 0 0		£ . 0 0

Calculating your taxable profits

Your taxable profit may not be the same as your net profit. Please read the 'Self-employment (short) notes' to see if you need to make any adjustments and fill in the boxes which apply to arrive at your taxable profit for the year.

27	Goods and/or services for your own use - read the notes	29	Loss brought forward from earlier years set off against this year's profits - up to the amount in box 28
	£ . 0 0		£ . 0 0
28	Net business profit for tax purposes (if box 21 + box 26 + box 27 minus (boxes 22 to 25) is positive)	30	Any other business income not included in box 9 or box 10 - for example, non arm's length reverse premiums
	£ . 0 0		£ . 0 0

Total taxable profits or net business loss

If your total profits from all Self-employments and Partnerships for 2016–17 are less than £5,965, you do not have to pay Class 2 National Insurance contributions, but you may want to pay voluntarily (box 36) to protect your rights to certain benefits. Read the notes.

31	Total taxable profits from this business (if box 28 + box 30 minus box 29 is positive)	32	Net business loss for tax purposes (if boxes 22 to 25 minus (box 21 + box 26 + box 27) is positive)
	£ . 0 0		£ . 0 0

Losses, Class 2 and Class 4 National Insurance contributions (NICs) and CIS deductions

If you have made a loss for tax purposes (box 32), read the 'Self-employment (short) notes' and fill in boxes 33 to 35 as appropriate.

33	Loss from this tax year set off against other income for 2016–17	36	If your total profits for 2016–17 are less than £5,965 and you choose to pay Class 2 NICs voluntarily, put 'X' in the box - read the notes
	£ . 0 0		
34	Loss to be carried back to previous year(s) and set off against income (or capital gains)	37	If you are exempt from paying Class 4 NICs, put 'X' in the box - read the notes
	£ . 0 0		
35	Total loss to carry forward after all other set-offs - including unused losses brought forward	38	Total Construction Industry Scheme (CIS) deductions taken from your payments by contractors - CIS subcontractors only
	£ . 0 0		£ . 0 0

Boxes from the Top upto number 8 are for personal information about the owner and their business. The software generates **Report A1** as the Short Tax Return, to provide figures for filling in the **Tax Report or Return**. Below is an illustration for Tiny Shop;

TINY SHOP	
Jan-2017 to Dec-2017	
SHORT TAX RETURN - SA103S	
Business Income	**To Notes**
9 Your Turnover ⓘ	33,570.90
10 Other Business Income ⓘ	0.00
Allowable Business Expenses	
11 Cost of Goods for Resale or Used ⓘ	22,535.00
12 Car, Van and Travel Expenses	0.00
13 Wages, Salaries and Other Staff Costs	0.00
14 Rent, Rates, Power and Insurance Costs	0.00
15 Repairs and Renewals of Property & Equipment	0.00
16 Accountacy, Legal and Other Professional Fees	0.00
17 Interest, Bank, Credit Card, Financial Charges	0.00
18 Phone, Fax, Stationery and Other Office Costs	0.00
19 Other Allowable Business Expenses	0.00
20 Total Expenses ⓘ	22,535.00
21 **Net Profit before Adjustment**	11,035.90
22 Net Loss before Adjustment	0.00
23 Annual Investment Allowance	0.00
24 Other Allowances ⓘ	0.00
25 Written Down Allowances	0.00
26 Balancing Charge	0.00
27 Personal Goods & Services	0.00
28 Net Profit 4 Tax Purposes	11,035.90
29 Loss B/F	
30 Income Not in box 9 & 10	
31 **Total Taxable Profit**	11,035.90
32 Net Loss 4 Tax Purposes	0.00
33 Loss against Other Income	Consult
34 Loss to Previous Years if ceased.	Consult
35 Loss C/F ⓘ	0.00
36 Tick box to calculate Voluntary NIC 2 ⓘ	☐
37 Tick box if Excepted from paying NIC 4	ⓘ ☐
38 CIS Tax Deducted	0.00

This report is accessed by tapping 9 Reports, then Year End Reports, then A Tax Accounts Reports, and finally A1 Short Tax Return. **Please Note that this A1 report can be customized to satisfy the requirements in other countries.**

The numbering of the boxes matches the actual Tax Return, to reduce the task to **just copying figures** onto the actual Tax Return before submission to the Tax Authority. The figures in **boxes 9 and 10** are copied onto the actual Tax Return.

There is a notice just above box 11, "If your Annual Turnover was **below £83,000** (implying Not Vat Registered), you may just put your Total Expenses in box 20, rather than filling in the whole section".

This is the reason why we advise that **all Allowable Expenses** can be recorded onto **account 25.** Basing on Report A1, we copy Total Expenses into **box 11**, and the same figure into **box 20** since there is nothing else to add. We copy the Net Profit before Adjustments into **box 21**, and the same figure into **box 28 and 31**. The rest of the boxes are Not covered on this module. **Report A2** has the detailed calculations including the Tax amount and **Personal Tax Allowance** which are covered on Module 2 and 4.

Chapter 18   SUMMARY RECORDING GUIDE

For a better appreciation of the whole process, you are encouraged to record all the documents again. If you are using the Free version then simply un-install the App. **Re-install** and it comes with a fresh set of blank Accounts. If you are using the Paid App, Tap button **1K New Business** found in the **Settings** section. We assume you are familiar with the App at this stage. Below are the documents and recording Guide;

PRACTICE DOCUMENTS & GUIDES
Business Name: **Tiny Shop; (Use form 1A)** Financial Year is **Jan to Dec. Use 1B to Set Recording Date 30 Dec.** Add stock items, Record Documents, then check reports: **Annual General Ledger, C1 Trial Balance, ST1, ST5, ST11, ST13, B4, B1 & B2, Cash Register, Dashboard, and A1 Tax Report.**

Guiding Principle: Every Value TO: an account, **must come FROM:** an account.

Recording Guide

Classification	Form	Accounts	Items	Sell Price
Add Stock	1C	1201	Sony	321.20
Item Accounts		1202	Nokia	543.40
Sell Price from Doc 3		1203	Iphone	386.10
Re-Order Qty is 5 each		1204	Galaxy	272.80

Tiny Shop		1
Receipt Date:		01-Dec
For:	Owner's Investment	
2E	**Amount**	19,000.00
Rcvd by:	Cash	

Recording Guide

Doc	Classification	Form	2 Accounts	Is it Auto Selected?
1	Cash	2E	Top - Account **TO**	Select Ac 212
	Capital		Account **FROM**	YES - Ac 271

FUN Mobiles			2
RECEIPT	To: Tiny Shop		
	Stock	Date:	30-Dec
Items	**Price**	**QTY**	**Net Cost**
Sony	125.00	25	3,125.00
Nokia	309.00	25	7,725.00
Iphone	147.00	25	3,675.00
Galaxy	88.00	30	2,640.00
3C	**Total Amount**		17,165.00
Paid by:	Cash		

Recording Guide

Doc	Classification	Form	2 Accounts	Is it Auto Selected?
2	Stock	3C	Top - Account **TO**	Select Ac 25
	Purchase		Account **FROM**	YES - Ac 212
		Add Stock Rows		Select Items

The customers Paid 33,600, and the change amount was displayed.

TINY SHOP   ③

Cash Sales RECEIPT

Date: 30-Dec

Items	Price	QTY	Net Cost
Sony	321.20	18	5,781.60
Nokia	543.40	24	13,041.60
Iphone	386.10	17	6,563.70
Galaxy	272.80	30	8,184.00

3A   **Total Amount**   33,570.90

Paid by: Cash

Recording Guide

Doc	Classification	Form	2 Accounts	Is it Auto Selected?
3	Stock	3A	Top - Account **TO**	YES - Ac 212
	Sales		Account **FROM**	Select Ac 5
		Add Stock Rows		Select Items

Natwest Bank   ④

Deposit Slip No: 56

Date: 30-Dec

2C   **Cash Total**   29,200.00

Recording Guide

Doc	Classification	Form	2 Accounts	Is it Auto Selected?
4	Cash	2C	Top - Account **TO**	Select Ac 205
	Deposit		Account **FROM**	Select Ac 212

LOAN AGREEMENT   ⑤   **LN: 743**

Borrower: Tiny Shop   **Date:** 01-Dec

To Bank Account

Amount: 1,200.00 7A   **Period:** 12 Months

31-Dec

Monthly Interest: 30.00   2F **Monthly Total Repayment:**   130.00

Total Interest: 360.00   **Repayments Start:**   31-Dec

Recording Guide

Doc	Classification	Form	2 Accounts	Is it Auto Selected?
5	Loan	7A	Top - Account **TO**	YES - Ac 205
	Borrowed		Account **FROM**	Select Ac 225

Recording Guide

Doc	Classification	Form	2 Accounts	Is it Auto Selected?
5	Loan	2F	Top - Account **TO**	Select Ac 25
	Interest		Account **FROM**	Select Ac 225

Tiny Shop
Payment Voucher   ⑥
Date: 30-Dec
For: Personal Cash from Business
2D   Amount 12,000.00
Paid by: Bank

Recording Guide

Doc	Classification	Form	2 Accounts	Is it Auto Selected?
6	Personal	2D	Top - Account **TO**	YES - Ac 286
	Cash		Account **FROM**	Select Ac 205

Landlord   ⑦
Receipt   Date: 01-Dec
Details: Rent
2B   Amount   4,800.00
Paid by: Cash

Recording Guide

Doc	Classification	Form	2 Accounts	Is it Auto Selected?
7	Rent	2B	Top - Account **TO**	YES - Ac 25
			Account **FROM**	YES - Ac 212

Natwest Bank   ⑧
CASH WITHDRAW Slip
2C   Date: 30-Dec
Account Number   774174
Name: Tiny Shop
Amount   120.00
Signature: _____

Recording Guide

Doc	Classification	Form	2 Accounts	Is it Auto Selected?
8	Cash	2C	Top - Account **TO**	YES - Ac 212
	Withdraw		Account **FROM**	YES - Ac 205

PC Store	(9)
Receipt	**Date:** 01-Dec
Details: **Android Tablet**	
	Net Amount 450.00
2B	**Vat** 90.00
	Total 540.00
Paid by: Bank	

Recording Guide

Doc	Classification	Form	2 Accounts	Is it Auto Selected?
9	Tablet PC	2B	Top - Account **TO**	YES - Ac 25
			Account **FROM**	Select Ac 205

Tiny Shop	(10)
Payment Voucher	
Date:	31-Dec
For: **Final Tax Paid**	
2F	**Amount** 1,500.00
Paid by: Cash	

Recording Guide

Doc	Classification	Form	2 Accounts	Is it Auto Selected?
10	Tax Paid	2F	Top - Account **TO**	Select Ac 281
			Account **FROM**	Select Ac 212

THE EXPECTED TRIAL BALANCE, AS A GUIDE

TINY SHOP	
Jan-2017 to Dec-2017	
ANNUAL TRIAL BALANCE	**ATB**
To Quarterly TB	**FINAL BALANCES**
5 All Income	-33,570.90
25 All Expenses	22,535.00
205 Bank1	17,740.00
212 Cash	25.90
225 Loan1	-1,230.00
271 Capital Added	-19,000.00
281 Final Tax Paid	1,500.00
286 Owner Cash Before Tax	12,000.00
Difference To Investigate	**0.00**

This practice can be done as many times as you wish. Those who prefer a different set of records may request via our WhatsApp contact. This is the start of building up **basic experience.**

Chapter 19   <u>MODULE 2 OVERVIEW</u>

Business Owners, Managers, and Supervisors are encouraged Not to end at Module 1 but acquire the **skills, exposure,** and **build on experience** provided n **Module 2.** It provides a much better understanding of what is done in the Bookkeeping and Accounting functions of a business. **Trainee Accountants and Bookkeepers** are encouraged to progress to Module 4, let alone Module 8.

The 1 Day Accounts is followed by **Module 2, Small Business Accounts,** summarised below;

<u>Assumptions Followed</u>
1. A Personal business Not Vat Registered
2. Fixed Assets used for only 2 Years, recorded as Expenses
3. No Year End Adjustments
4. **Incomes & Expenses Analysed**
5. Single File for All Documents

<u>M2 COVERAGE</u>
<u>M1 Documents & Procedures Repeated</u>

1) Adding Stock Items	5) Cash Deposit & Withdraw
2) Money Capital	6) Personal Cash Taken
3) Stock Purchases	7) Fixed Asset & Rent Paid
4) Stock & Point of Sale	8) Loan Borrowed & Interest

<u>M2 Extra Documents & Procedures</u>

1) New Business	15) Wages without Tax
2) Customising Bank Account	16) Tax Debt Paid
3) Stock Purchase Refund	17) Tax Assessed
4) Stock Sales Refund	18) Credit Card Reconciliation
5) Stock Transportation	19) Credit Card Repaid & Interest
6) Naming Creditor Accounts	20) Loan Reconciliation
7) Naming Debtor Accounts	21) Loan Repaid
8) Opening Balances	22) Bank Reconciliation
9) Opening Tax Debt	23) Bank Interest Income
10) Opening Creditors & Debtors	24) Bank Charges
11) Creditors & Debtors Paid	25) Previous Year Comparison
12) Credit Stock Sales	26) Previous Year Creditors
13) Expense Invoices	27) Previous Year Debtors
14) Cancelled Sale	28) Backup anc Restore

M1 Reports Repeated

1) The Ledger - AGL
2) Trial Balance
3) Stock Information
4) Stock Movement
5) Annual Stock Sales & Profit
6) Stock Taking List
7) Cash Register
8) Notes to Financial Statements
9) Profit and Loss Account
10) Balance Sheet
11) Tax Report
12) Owner's Income Calculation

M2 Stock Management Reports

1) Daily Stock Sales
2) Stock Sales by Item
3) Monthly Stock Sales & Profit
4) Monthly Stock Ledger
5) Daily Stock Purchases
6) Stock Purchases by Item
7) Cummulative Stock Bought
8) Stock Bought & Average Costs
9) Annual Stock Ledger
10) Supplier Statement
11) Customer Statement

M2 Extra Reports

1) Mini YE Reports Checklist
2) Bank & Loan Reconciliation
3) Credit Card Reconciliation
4) Bank Summary and Reconciliation
5) Last Bank Statement
6) Bank Account
7) Cash Summary & Reconciliation
8) Cash Account
9) Debtors Summary & Reconciliation
10) Debtor's Control Account
11) Annual Debtor's Ledger
12) Creditors Summary & Reconciliation
13) Creditors Control Account
14) Annual Creditors Ledger
15) Loan Summary & Reconciliation
16) Last Loan Statements
17) Loan Account
18) Credit Card Summary & Reconciliation
19) Last Credit Card Statement
20) Credit Card Account

Support

In case of any questions please contact us via **WhatsApp** +44 7415 618 342 or **Lite Facebook Messenger, & Facebook**

Alternative contacts are; admin@practicalaccounts.com, and mosesbak@yahoo.co.uk

www.ingramcontent.com/pod-product-compliance
Lightning Source LLC
Chambersburg PA
CBHW071224220526
45468CB00002B/725